How To Validate Your Startup Business Idea?

By

Ravi Kikan

© All Copyrights Reserved, 2018

This book is dedicated to all the hustlers who are trying to dent our blue planet with new business ideas,

Including You :)

e-Meet-Ravi Kikan (Author)

I advise startups for growth.

I love startups & my experience across sectors like Media & PR, Fintech, Education, Advertising, Retail, Mobile, Healthcare, AI, iOT, Tech, e-commerce has helped me to launch startups & grow ventures into profitable hubs. I love working with global entrepreneurs, startups, community builders, institutions and investors.Have been instrumental in strategising, building and running startup operations in a CXO advisory role along with leading cross functional teams across geographies. I run some of the largest startup communities on LinkedIn. I am the group owner and moderator for two of the largest groups on LinkedIn & Facebook:

Startup Specialists https://www.linkedin.com/groups/56766 is one of the largest moderated group for startups amid the 2 million+ groups on LinkedIn. Around 300,000 global startups/entrepreneurs discuss & create invaluable content.

Oscarinus https://www.facebook.com/groups/oscarinus is the largest moderated support group with around 30,000 members on Facebook who support Oscar Pistorius.

I also love mentoring startups, incubators and also take lectures in various B schools covering topics on entrepreneurship, growth & marketing.

How To Validate Your Startup Business Idea is my compilation of thoughts and experiences on how anyone who is thinking of starting a new startup business should validate the new business idea before going all out in the market and reach his or her set target goals.

I also look forward to your feedback and support to spread the good word and help any budding entrepreneur validate his or her startup business idea.

Connect & Follow Me Here:

Twitter : https://twitter.com/ravikikan
LinkedIn: https://www.linkedin.com/in/ravikikan

Index

1. My Digital Community Experience
2. Global Experts & Rockstars
3. Why This Book ?
4. The Rabbit Hole
5. Who Is This Book For ?
6. How To Use This Book ?
7. Introduction
8. Basic Definitions That You Should Know
9. Background
10. Basic Level Business Validation Process
11. Chit Chat With Experts
12. Global Point Of View (POV)
13. THE GIST: Global POV
14. The Final Revision
15. Final Pointers, Let's Revise
16. A Little Prayer (Note To Self)

My Digital Community Experience

As I shared with you I run some of the largest digital communities for startups and entrepreneurs on LinkedIn. The best part of leading a big digital startup global community is always getting a global perspective on things and issues. I have time and again participated in some awesome discussions with entrepreneurs/startups and also reached out to global experts.

These global experts are successful VCs, Entrepreneurs, Angel Investors, Startup Specialists, Advisors or Mentors who have seen the startup ecosystem more closely than others, so taking their opinion and point of view of the subject meant sharing with you (the reader) a global perspective on the topic so that you wouldn't have go it anywhere else but have a regional and global understanding.

The second biggest thing that I learnt while handling digital communities is that networking with people from across the world is very important. You tend to learn so many things that otherwise you would not have ever learnt if you were limited to your own geographies.

The best part of picking up brains from across the world is also to give a heads up to you in terms of the various criticisms, hurdles, challenges, aspects that they have faced or seen in their careers and experiences. These might differ from geography to geography. So the experiences are myriad in nature and bring out most of the aspects that someone might face while starting up his or her own venture especially at the business validation stage.

Last not the least is the power of unlearning what you have learnt and relearning new things. This means that you should be willing to adopt to new learnings only once you are receptive and willing to learn new ways of doing things by overwriting or adding to your existing line of thinking.

Be willing to unlearn and relearn :)

Notes That You Should Take

- Learn from the startup community
- Be a part of the startup ecosystem to learn
- Take myriad views from everyone
- Invest on networking
- Check Experiences Of People Around You
- Take Criticism In The Right Spirit
- Check All Perspectives
- Be Willing To Unlearn and Relearn

Global Experts and Rockstars

Let me Thank The Startup Rockstars, Bowing Down To The Startup Ecosystem Around You.

I have collated my thoughts and experiences from the startups and enterprises that I have worked with. I also take this opportunity to thank some awesome global professionals who have contributed their thoughts in building this book. This book will be extremely helpful for entrepreneurs, startups and wanna be startup specialists who are on the planning stage to validate their business idea. I would love to thank the following extraordinary startup GLOBAL ROCKSTARS without whom this book wouldn't have been possible. These are the people who are startup rockstars in their own domain and some of them took out time and shared their point of view on what they feel is right on the subject. These are the global experts who have been investors, entrepreneurs, mentors, startup specialists, coaches who have been there and done that thing time and again.

It is extremely important when you are going down an unknown path that you collect experiences of people who have been on that path or similar paths in life. What that experience gives you is that **immeasurable high** that you might not get from elsewhere else.

Thank You Global Rockstars, Each One Of You !

Praval Kant, Tina Zurbi, Neeraj Saini, Sandeep Balaji, Diana Palchik, Dr Aniruddha Malpani, Rajiv Tewari, Joseph Roos, Avigail Berg, Ed Frankel, Patrick Osman, Tishana Simon, Pranab Sen, Nitin Jain, Ed Zimmer, Andrea Sica, Zile Soilihi, Jeffrey Hilton, Guy Cleveland, Richard Coleness, Tabitha Jean Naylor, Andrew McWhirter, Matt Kurleto, Daniel Leping.

P.s: Always Thank The Ecosystem :)

Why This Book ?

Knowing that Rabbit Hole

"If You Don't Know Where You Are Going, Any Road Will Get You There"

Alice In Wonderland

Your business idea is your conceived baby, you need to handle it well and you need to ensure it is born in the right environment and is incubated well for a better growth.

So technically you are the guardian of your business idea, still better, the parent :)

There are many reasons how this book can be useful to you HOWEVER the best reason is that it will help you to get reach your business validation process. This seems to me the biggest reason why I work with entrepreneurs and startups. **NO ONE can guarantee success or failure however the only thing you can do is increase the chances of success by planning it in the right way and executing it.**

Remember both PLANNING and EXECUTING are equally important.

Sometimes in the enlightenment of the business idea or in the haste of getting things done faster with shortcuts (Howsoever the idea might be great), we end up doing the following :

1. We forget the simple basics
2. We tend to overlook similar experiences
3. We do not take stable advises
4. We rush into getting things done faster
5. We often get misguided

6. We overlook readily available data
7. We sometimes ONLY look at money and not the business process
8. We don't validate things before going all out

Time and again I have seen my friends, colleagues, awesome entrepreneurs, startups (including myself) that the biggest reason of getting into a new business without the validation of the idea has let to extremely disastrous and sometimes fatal outcomes. Lot of things get on stake e.g. like your time, money, resources, relationships, career etc. So it is always a sane idea that we dig a little deeper into things before jumping into that Alice in Wonderland Rabbit hole...where we actually have some fair idea what we can expect on the other side of the tunnel.

The Rabbit Hole- The Unknown Journey

The whole objective is for you to know the path you are going and what you might expect on that path. Jumping onto an unknown runway where you don't know where it would lead and what you might expect onway might seems adventurous but then it is more of a guessing game. Lot of things are at stake when you start your business so you better be prepared with some questions and answers yourself so that you are well prepared for your business journey.

Not just because your best friend told you to start a great idea or for that matter your saw an existing gap in the market that you wanted to fulfill....The idea can be great but it still needs some validation before it goes live in the market. If you don't do a fact check you might regret in what you could have done to get your validations for business idea before it went live.

You ALWAYS learn from mistakes but don't repeat them.

Yes agree. Lot of entrepreneurs & startups, time and again have done this mistake and have learnt from it. Your business idea validation with some facts and figures could save you all of that and what you do in that process is extremely critical. The initial hard work that you put in for your idea validation makes the base of the your whole business. There are often many ways you can do the same. The validation might differ from the sector to sector however the basics will remain the same. Learn from those basics, Learn from the success, failures, mistakes and experiences from people who have been there and done that time and again. It will not only save you time but money, burnout and stress.

Notes That You Should Take
"Reduce Your Chances Of Failure And Increase Your Chances Of Success"

- Don't Forget The Basics
- Don't Overlook Similar Experiences
- Do Take Stable Advises
- Don't Rush Into Getting Things Done Faster
- Don't Get Misguided
- Don't Overlook Readily Available Data
- Don't ONLY Look At Money But Also The Business Process

" Mistakes Are Meant For Learning. Not Repeating."

--- Anonymous

Who Is This Book For ?

This is exactly what you should ideally be reading before you jump all out in the market to start your own business or your startup. This is irrespective whether you want to start a product or services based business.

This book is ideal for someone who is :

1. Thinking or planning to start his or her own business
2. Has an idea for business but doesn't know what to do with it
3. Has an idea but is currently not sure how to go forward
4. Wanting to validate his or her business idea
5. Fearful to start a business because of the fear of failure

So irrespective whether you are *a student, a budding entrepreneur, a homemaker, a retired professional, a corporate employee with a great idea or planning to launch a new product/services, a bunch of friends thinking about a possible solution to an existing problem or issue, a startup who has thought about a product or service....*This is your book for validation of your startup business idea.

This is also **YOUR** book if you are someone who is planning to start e.g. your own tuition centre, your e-commerce store, build an Ed Tech startup for school going kids, a mobile app , your own consulting practice, a digital marketing company, a technology venture etc there is no harm in preparing yourself in the business you are venturing in.

You also need to understand three very important things :

1. Remember YOUR STARTUP IDEA is your own baby or your own small sapling that you need to nurture HOWEVER you need to ensure that it is incubated well in the right circumstances and at the right time and often at the right place. Not all variants might be conducive to you

HOWEVER you need to ensure you have validated all possibilities so that you are prepared for the outcomes.

2. Ideally have a conducive environment around you to work on your business idea. Most often than not we hurry into doing things whether an assignment, work deadline or for that matter business as well. This might come handy at times for some lucky people but doesn't work in a bigger ratio. So if you are someone on the verge or incubating your business idea or someone who is still in the planning stage, reach out to your critics, friends, family, professionals, entrepreneurs who might give you some insider tips on the business that you are about to launch. They may have a different point of view for all the things that you are planning to do but there is no harm listening to everyone and evaluating the various parameters to avoid any future pitfalls. So listen and evaluate :)

3. Please take the feedback of your Critics and Mentors with a pinch of salt. Not everyone will give you accolades for your million dollar idea. You best friend or an investor might just tear through your business idea by giving you 10 reason why you should not venture into that particular business idea HOWEVER if you have already explored the answers or you have a strong data to support on why you should venture into it then it makes a lot of sense. There will be people who will ask and question you on your idea validation. **You do not have to emotionally react or think about those critical remarks but you need to see your idea into light keeping those pointers in mind**. No harm revisiting your idea board time and again before your launch, you never know what all you could be missing.

Yes no harm in getting people around you who can motivate you to start something exciting but in the heat of the moment you should carry your head along with you when you are investing through your heart :)

Build Your Business Idea Board

Write down your idea and various questions regarding your startup business idea on a Business Idea Board and revisit it every day with the relevant answers to all the queries. This **Business Idea Board** could be a whiteboard or a pin board on your working desk.

You will be surprised at the kind of questions that you would be bouncing on each day when you start thinking or validating your business idea with different parameters and the awesome answers that you will get or explore or dig in your business validation journey.

" I Am Not A Product Of My CircumStances, I Am A Product Of My Decisions"

--- Stephen Covey

Notes That You Should Take

"Build A Business Idea Board"

- Validate Your All Options
- Don't Hurry In Any Process
- Be Prepared For Outcomes
- Take Constant Feedbacks
- Take Criticism Proactively
- Listen and Evaluate
- Don't Have A Fear Of Failure
- Plan Where To Start From

"Who Is This Book For?"

- Thinking or planning to start his or her own business
- Has an idea for business but doesn't know what to do with it
- Has an idea but is currently not sure how to go forward
- Wanting to validate his or her business idea
- Fearful to start a business because of the fear of failure
- Students Aspiring To Be Entrepreneurs
- Budding Entrepreneurs
- Wannabe Startups
- Homemakers
- Professionals
- Corporates Wanting To Launch New Products

"Don't Believe Everything You Think, Validate It"

---- Anonymous

"If Your Work Isn't Fun, You Are Not Playing In The Right Team"

---- Frank Sonnenberg

How To Use This Book ?

The entire content in this book is built on the examples and experiences I have had with global experts, entrepreneurs & startup specialists. Entrepreneurs have tasted success and failures and you get to learn a hell lot from them. A lot of hard work has gone in building this content so that YOU can reach your success point in whatever you are planning to do but start first with validating your startup business idea.

My own experiences of success and failures have been very helpful in building and asking critical questions that might be relevant for all budding startups and entrepreneurs who are planning to validate their startup business ideas.

My objective has been simple, to reach out to you and share with you how best you can validate your business idea and startup your venture with a bang.Keep in mind your focus at all times when you are going through this book will be to evaluate your startup business idea and keep validating your assumptions with factual data. While many case studies etc will be discussed in the book however you keep your mind focussed on your business idea so that you are streamlined on your business validation process.

You do not need to be an expert to understand things but yes no harm in learning from experts. Here is how I suggest you should enjoy this book and learn from reading it:

- Think about the business idea which you want to start
- Create your Business Idea Board
- Keep a diary and pen ready with you
- Write down each key point from every page you read from this book
- Validate with your business idea at every point along with whatever you have read
- Write down points that you do not understand or want to understand
- Go back and re-read the pointers and try answering those questions

- Validate with your business idea at every point
- Do not loose the grip of the business idea that you want to validate
- UnLearn and ReLearn

" Start Where You Are, Use What You Have, Do What You Can "

--- Arthur Ashe

" Be Stubborn On Your Vision But Flexible On Details"

---- Jeff Bezos

Notes That You Should Take
"Keep Validating Your Startup Business Idea"

- Take Notes
- Write Questions
- Use Your **Business Idea Board**
- Ask Questions
- Look for all Answers
- Try Finding Out Solutions
- Unlearn and Relearn
- Take Taking Notes
- Keep Focussed on Your Business Idea

" *The Key To Success Is To Start Before You Are Ready* "

---- Marie Forleo

" *Sometimes The Biggest Step In The Right Direction Ends Up Being The Biggest Step In Your Life* "

---- Steve Maraboli

" *Winning Means You Are Willing To Go Longer, Work Harder And Give More Than Anyone Else* "

---- Vince Lombardi

" *People Inspire You or They Drain You, Pick Them Wisely* "

---- Hans F Hanson

Introduction To Basics

Let's start from here now. Great if you already have a startup business idea.

This is the first thing.

It is advisable to work with passion on the same startup idea and build a startup business from it. **Ideally your startup business idea should be from any of these 5 buckets** :

1. It is currently solving a real world problem
2. It is aiming to bridge an existing gap in the market
3. You plan to build economies of scale
4. You plan to create a new market altogether (disrupt/innovation)
5. There is an actual NEED for your product i.e. There is an addressable market/customers (large) for your product/services

So write down which among the above is the right bucket for your business idea ? Keep your mind aligned towards it. Your idea becomes extremely strong if it falls in many buckets.

You can choose or brainstorm to build your idea majorly from any of the above categories however keep your mind and heart working in tandem. You need to assess the startup idea from all directions before you really jump into the the business. Nothing wrong in that.

The Second Thing.

The second most important thing is that you **CANNOT** afford to jump into a new business till the time you haven't done a realistic fact check on how feasible is the idea for a business. If you haven't done the feasibility study for the business idea you are surely asking for trouble. Time and again entrepreneurs with great ideas have fallen flat as they did not do a last mile check or never went into the details of the feasibility of the business idea.

This is where both hard work and smart work comes into play. This is where most people fail. Take a note of this.

This ebook has been made keeping in mind that how an average person looks at a startup idea and what all he or she needs to actually prepare to valid that business idea before he or she goes all out in the market with all guns blazing.

" Whatever The Problem, Be Part Of The Solution "

--- Tina Fey

Notes That You Should Take

"Be Realistic, Ideally Your Idea Should Be From Any Of These 5 Buckets or *The Best Case Scenario*, It Falls Into All These 5 Buckets"

- It is currently solving a real world problem
- It is aiming to bridge an existing gap in the market
- You plan to build economies of scale
- You plan to create a new market altogether (disrupt/innovation)
- There is an actual NEED for your product i.e. There is an addressable market/customers (large) for your product/services

" Your Job Isn't To make Money. It's To Find The Problem That Needs Solving"

--- Robert. T. KiyoSaki

" If You Are Not Willing To Learn, No One Can Help You. If You Are Determined To Learn Than No One Can Stop You"

---- Anonymous

" Believe You Can And You're Halfway There "

---- Theodore Roosevelt

Basic Definitions You Should Know

If you are wanting to become a product company or wanting to launch some new services in the market and looking for business idea validation than these definitions would come very handy.

But before we dig deep, we should know the following :

- MVP (Minimum Viable Product)
- Prototype
- Proof Of Concept (POC)

So what is a MVP ?

A MVP (Minimum Viable Product) is a product version which has very basic features for early adopting customers which you can pitch it to them and get initial feedback for product enhancement and development. This connotation as I shared earlier is generally used in the software and SaaS companies.

You have to keep in mind that a MVP has to be just functional early stage product which can be used by the customers which means it can be sold to the customers and is saleable. A MVP doesn't have to be a perfect full product offering.

An MVP also gives an opportunity to you to test your product features, usage with the customers and get a chance to have scope of improvements. This helps you to mitigate the risk of launching a fully functional complete product and incur costs, time and energy if it fails.

The whole purpose of a MVP is to look into the following things :

1. Test the product early in the market
2. Fast Go To Market Launch
3. Faster Learning on the product and market

4. Reduce risk of failure
5. Reduce load on technology
6. Have a scope to improve the product continuously

So what is a Prototype ?

A Prototype is an first version sample or a model release of a product which is built to test a hypothesis or a concept built for a duplicate to be shown. This term is widely used in the hardware, electronics, robotic, iOT, design including software programming.
Prototyping is measured for real working systems and used for evaluation for new design process to be used by users and analysts.

The whole purpose of a Prototyping is to look into the following things for a prospective design :

1. A visual prototype is like an engineering drawing for the product which shows the appearance and interface of the product. This is more User Interface focussed.
2. A working Prototype is a completely or near complete functional copy of the product in the final stage.
3. A User Experience Prototype is built keeping in mind the visual and functionality of the product. Combination of the above two technically.

What is POC ?

Proof Of Concept (POC) is a demonstration in practice of the feasibility of an idea in theory or practical to potentially launch it in the market in the right target audience.

It gives the probability if a product or service has a scope of acceptability in the customers that it has been designed for. It is a verifying & feasibility check stage.

The whole purpose of a POC is to look into the following things :

1. Verifying the concept or theory
2. Check the feasibility of the product or service launch
3. Is drivin my data which mostly is primary in nature
4. It may not be a complete product or service offering but an initial idea or concept with some basic outlay to support

Notes That You Should Take
"Test Fast, Test Early, Test Right"

- *Test The Feasibility Of The Idea*
- *Test The Feasibility In The Target Audience*
- *Does Your Target Audience Really Need Your Product/Services ?*
- *Build a POC and get ratification*
- *Get Your Market Data*
- *Build A MVP/ProtoType and Launch*

" Sell The Problem You Solve Not The Product "

--- Anonymous

Background

We often get business ideas….all of us,

some of them are weird,
some of them are feasible,
some of the are disruptive,
some are problem solvers,

Some of them are for mass consumption…and some are for specific needs and so on but how are you are sure that your startup business idea is validated for success ?

This is the question that has been haunting on me for quite some time both in terms of my experiences, in both success and failures. While everyone has a different opinion on this subject but it is always good to know some basics from experts or successful entrepreneurs who have been there and done that. **This reduces drastically the ratio of failure for your business idea going down the drain and all your hard work being flushed.**

I spoke and discussed this with a lot of global entrepreneurs, startups and industry veterans on the startup business idea validation and came out with some pointers and ideas that could help entrepreneurs and startups about to begin their journey or have started their journey and are at their idea stage.

As an entrepreneur you might be hounded by a million ideas for your business but actually how many of them would be worth it ? This will keep hounding you till you actually make your ideas turn into a product or service and put them into use/ market. Some of the business ideas may not be completely viable however some of them may have great potential.

Great.

Now the biggest challenge is : How Do You Evaluate An Idea for Startup Business ?

There is no fixed answer to this however if you are a little proactive and can listen to some friends, family or serial entrepreneurs...chances are that your ideas can be evaluated, tested and put into use.My personal experience is testing and building a MVP (Minimum Viable Product). This is especially important if you are a product company e.g. if you have a SaaS based product.

Once you test the MVP with the actual customers you can evaluate your idea. You will know whats the demand of your product with the actual customers and not just fictitious forecasting on paper. You take feedbacks from your actual customers and go back to table to fine tune your product and bring it back on the table. So you are doing two things, improving your product and validating at the same time. This is real business validation. We shall discuss this in detail in the various sections of this book.

Notes That You Should Take

"Take An Opinion From Experts or Entrepreneurs Who Have Walked This Journey Before"

- Evaluate The Idea
- Test The Idea
- Put The Idea Into The Market
- Prefer Real Market Feedback
- Do Primary & Secondary Research
- Get Back, Refine The Product/Services

*" The Most Important Thing In Communication Is **Hearing** What Isn't Said"*

--- Peter Drucker

*" People Don't Care About Your Business. They Care About Their Problems. Be The **Solution** That They Are Looking For "*

--- Melonie Dodaro

*" Success Is Not Delivering A Feature, It Is **Learning** How To Solve The Customer's Problem "*

--- Eric Ries

Basic Level Validation Process

We need to dig in a more a little to understand these concepts from a user perspective and not just fancy lexicons out of the tech world :)

It's about the growth stage of your startup and not just your product

E.g. When you develop or think of an 'app as a great idea' you have basically hunted for a gap or a problem fixing solution and the best way what you feel to cover the gap or to solve the problem is building that app and growing it fast, really fast so that you can reach out to the maximum consumers in a shortest span of time and increasing your business reach and growth.

From the above presumption and vision every venture kicks off at the POC stage. It is the same process of validating your assumptions and your complete business model of how you have thought it to be. It can range from a diversified research , data assumptions to more manual interventions like building pre sales funnels, inquiries to demo the scope of your business AKA " **solution to the big gap or problem**"

So what should we call the Version 1.0 of your product ?

In building through this process e.g. for a software or hardware product "a total visual representation of the product which can be shown through wireframes and in a pictorial mode focussing on the UX/UI and still not being functional with some live data will be a prototype version"

This I call is the "Simulation Mode"

E.g. in a tech startup, as soon as the User Experience & Design team can build a prototype which can demo the process and stages of the product from end to end without still in the coding stage, you can always bring this on your feedback table with the actual users to correct the shortcuts and products lacunas.

At this stage no code has gone into the product thus the cost of development is saved for optimizing the product as per the Target Audience. So big changes could be made at no extra costs at this prototyping stage itself and the product could be refined over again.

Once this is ready with all corrections, the prototype can be handed over to the development teams with instructions, playbook for the product and the prototype is ready to convert into the MVP (Minimum Viable Product)

Building the MVP/Prototype & Go To Market Planning

A minimum viable product AKA "MVP" is a fully operational, go to market product that has been built for the consumption of the early adopters & stakeholders (AKA consumers) and suffices the market fit and opportunity gap in the optimum way.

This is more conducive for startups that are planning to launch a product.

An alternate definition also could be

"You can say it is a fully operational prototype coded which is live with the stakeholders and actual consumers built in with a constant loop of feedback for improvement to be in a state of continuous beta"

1. Continuous Beta would mean a basic MVP product that is evolving with constant feedback coming from Actual customers and Prospective Customers.

2. Don't wait for a perfect product, bring out your workable product in the market for continuous testing so that it keep evolving with feedbacks.
3. Customers should love the functionality and usage of the product, the other things like colors, design, fonts etc could keep evolving (User Interface)
4. Many startups and entrepreneurs spend too much time, human capital, money, energy and permutations to build a perfect product. This not only hampers the Go To Market Planning for the business but also delays the opportunity cost from the market.
5. There is nothing like a perfect product, every product is evolving and comes out with versions constantly.
6. Believe in going lean and fast to launch your product. Don't keep testing the product in your lab or office, Go out and take feedback as much as you can
7. Keep improving, Keep reaching out to more prospective consumers

So now comes the next set of questions :

- **What is your objective in this whole process ?**
- **Who is your right Target Audience ?**
- **Is your Target Audience beyond your consumers ?**
- **How are your pricing your product or services ?**

Validation of your startup business idea has to be with the right targeting, here are some few steps you should take into consideration :

1. You should first understand whom are you wanting to reach and for what purposes for your product or services E.g. If you are trying to build a prototype of an mobile APP than the UI/UX needs to be fixed, so it would be imperative that you first get to understand e.g. how will the customer want to see my app ?, what kind of color schemes would the app have, what kind of basic UX functionalities the product should

have, does these functionalities gel with the right TA (Target Audience) ? Keep testing it with various stakeholders and TA.
2. Validate the idea with the right target audience and stakeholders. This means that people who could be your possible customers and early adopters to use your product. E.g. if you have an app that will help locate kids around, do take out time to test the MVP or the prototype with parents in your vicinity, known schools, preschools, parents or your friends who have families and who might be willing to experiment and test your product.
3. With this you always have a chance to go back and fill the gaps that your product might need in the market whether the pointers are design related or functionality related either ways it will help your product.
4. This will also help you price the product appropriately for your target audience. They will have the right aptitude to tell you how much they are willing to shell out for the products or services
5. The other stakeholders could be investors, media etc who might want to test the product/service or have a look at the product/service. Reaching out to investors not for funds but only for feedback of your product or services gives you an edge of understanding how an investor might look into your product/service from an overall business validation point of view. This will also test how much validation and growth planning you have done in the market and for your business. They might be very critical on your business but that's fine, it ok to do learn and improve on your mistakes. Your reaching out to them gives you an edge in terms of being prepared for being investor friendly and PR friendly. You might also get some eyeballs in media and investment space. That's always an added advantage.

So now comes the next part of the question :
What results are you seeking through this orientation?

The next important element is to understand what validation are you seeking through the product build up process ?

1. **Is this the right product ?** If you are you at the POC stage than it is imperative that the concept needs to be validated first with the target audience at large before you go into any next stage. It is also imperative to understand that either there is a need, gap in the market or a total new disruptive market your are building with your product and your product falls into any of these 3 basic thumb rule categories.
2. **Will this product work fine ?** Once you are through the POC stage and now into the prototyping , wireframing stage of the product your validation ideally should be about the fixing of the UX and UI for the product. The more iterations with the TA and stakeholders that you do at this stage helps you in building a robust product and saves both time, energy and development cost.
3. **How will this product get acceleration & growth ?** Please understand you are doing a business and it is imperative that business building seeks revenues and sales. Once you are in the MVP stage and later when you go into public beta (full blown product live in TA) you should be doing critical growth tests for your products and tweaks to ensure the acceptability of the product is faster and to a wide mass audience. Your critical job here is to get the multiplier effect for the product. How fast and how many TA get to access my product and pay for.
4. **Who will help you in your growth and acceleration ?** Are you capacitized to handle the growth and acceleration for the product and services ? Do you have the ability and understanding ? Do you have the right human capital who can do it for you ? Are you prepared for this and have you planned the various phases ?

Yes you should have a plan for a superlative growth and quickly reaching your Rocket Point. Let's take an understanding of this growth point for a SaaS based company which needs product downloads.

The Tipping Point for Accelerated Product Downloads in a smaller time frame is The Rocket Point. You might want to detail the growhacking sessions once you have launched your product.

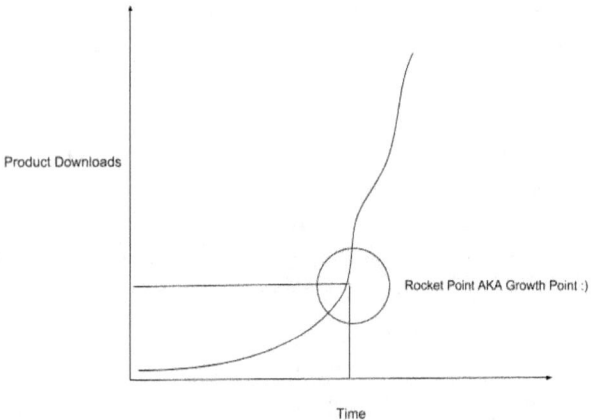

Notes That You Should Take

"Basic Level Business Idea Validation Requires You To Investigate Your Objectives, Target Audience And Launching Your Early Stage Product In The Market"

- Understand Who Are Your Targeting ?
- What Is The Objective Of Your Of Validation ?
- Understand Product, Market & Growth Parameters
- Getting The POC Done for Validation
- Building Your Prototype/MVP
- Learn About The Product & Take Feedback
- Will The Product Work Fine In The Target Audience ?
- Launching In The Target Audience
- How Are You Planning Growth & Acceleration For Your Product ?
- Who Will Help You In Your Growth ?

Chit Chat With Entrepreneurs

Here is one discussion between some global startup experts and entrepreneurs on "How to evaluate a startup business idea"

What are the main factors you may consider, to quickly evaluate a business idea?

A group of wonderful entrepreneurs from across the globe discussed this idea and came out with some wonderful insights which could be useful to you as a reader in understanding how your idea validation is important and can be done in easy, practical steps.

Ed Zimmer: "Quick" evaluation is worthless - might as well just flip a coin. Real evaluation: First, define who would buy what you're thinking of. Then, if B2C or B2B, find a way of meeting them - in-person (conferences, trade shows, cold calling, etc.). If B2C, primary source are manufacturers, distributors, retailers selling to your prospects, and meet them the same way. Good approach, "I'm thinking about doing such-and-such. What do you think?". And LISTEN.

You'll soon know whether the idea is worth pursuing - and if it is, you'll gain a whole new light on what it is you need to pursue

Andrea Sica : Thanks a lot Ed. A very practical and effective approach. Straight to the point! Yeah, I completely agree, listening your customers is one of the main points to evaluate whether the idea is really worth it taking to the market, and taking some changes in case. I would also be curious to know what a venture (or anyway investors) would think about it.

Ed Zimmer: Well, investors don't invest in IDEAS. They'll invest in PEOPLE with ideas. But what attracts them most is CUSTOMERS. If you have a couple of large contracts with established firms with a dozen more in the works, you'll have no difficulty finding investors. Likewise if you've been in business a couple of years and are showing an accelerating (profitable) customer set. But getting their investment back also comes into it. A general expectation among venture investors is that they'll be getting back (in cash) like 10 times their investment in a relatively short period like 3-5 years. And magnitude also comes into it.

VCs will make only very large investments. Angels will make medium-size investments. But no one will invest penny in expectation of a dollar return. I'd recommend staying away from investors, at least until you have a "customer" situation like I described above. If the idea is good, there's always a way to build a customer set with little investment.

Zile Soilihi: Try the business model canvas approach which is efficient even you don't have a bm yet. It helps you , iteratively ,ask the questions.. What is my "idea" value proposition ? Who are my customers and how do i engage them?..etc. How do i generate money ? etc.

Ed Zimmer: Zile. But that's why the small business failure rate is so high. When you ask complex questions - especially to yourself - you get complex (and useless) answers. The simple fact is no one going into business KNOWS what to expect. They may have constructed good arguments of how things should be, but even the luckiest find many flaws in the arguments they constructed - and those less lucky make up the failure statistics. The ONLY ones who know whether a business will work are your prospects - and it's absolute insanity not to spend considerable time conversing with them before even thinking about starting a business.

Zile Soilihi: True Ed. But when i'm talking about asking questions it's mainly to your PROSPECTS. This is what business model canvas is about. This why it's an iterative approach between the entrepreneur assumptions and the prospect needs you bring ...

Ed Zimmer: Zile. But who are the prospects? In B2C they're not the people who will end up with the product but the manufacturers, distributors, retailers that sell to those people (because they're the ones who you'll be selling to (and have best understanding of the particular market niche even if you decide to go direct). And once one KNOWS they have real prospective customers, what other questions are there other than "how can I supply what they're asking for at a price they'll pay". And I'm not going to sit down with a spreadsheet, canvas or any other "system" to figure that out - I'm going to work that out with my prospects.

BTW, I'm not against the ideas of Ries, Maurya, etc. They're great for some startups (a lot better than the old ways) - but not for all startups. (All the MBA words alone will turn most people off.)

Zile Soilihi: "How can i .....at a price they'll pay" is a good question, indeed. But it doesn't address the profitability and growth issues. IN addition it implies several other sub-questions. And you don't start a business just because people are ready to pay, right? you need more analysis .Forget spreadsheets , if you don't like them , forget BM canvas if you don't like it ! But at the end of the day you need to put figures somewhere, you need some data to bring your idea to the market.):

Andrea Sica: Hi Zile, thanks for serving the PM canvas on the tray. I agree, that's so far still the most powerful system I think one can use to keep the focus, and ask the right questions. And I don't honestly see a contrast in your opinions, as in both cases you stress the importance of the value perceived by the customers. Thanks.

Ed Zimmer: Zile. You're too structured (aka, inflexible). Business is about making money - not in creating a monument. If one can't find a way to profit at the price customers can pay, one just doesn't go into that business - big deal - and I could care less about growth - if it's there, I take it - if it isn't, who cares. I've had over 20 businesses over my career (all made money) and I've never analyzed, projected, etc. - never had too. When you have your customers working with you, there's no need for that.

Ravi Kikan: Build a MVP and test with the customers instead of getting too much iterations.

Jeffrey Hilton: My first question: "Would I buy it?"

Guy Cleveland: Hi Ed- I like your comment above, "The ONLY ones who know whether a business will work are your prospects - and it's absolute insanity not to spend considerable time conversing with them before even thinking about starting a business." I agree many people hold a singular perception about their product/service and never bounce it around enough to those you will eventually rely upon to buy.

Even when larger companies market research you still see a lot starting from a bias and try to "fit" response to confirm the bias.-- Perhaps a true measure?

Ed Zimmer: Guy. And that's the problem with the "big idea" approach to business. In my first post here where I urged Andrea to talk with his prospects, I stressed the word "listen". But when a person has an idea that they believe is good, maybe even great, it's next to impossible for them to "listen". Emotionally they want to "sell" the idea, convince others. Even when they try their best to be objective, they undervalue the negatives and over-value the positives. The MVP that Blank and Ries popularized is an attempt to get around this - put together the minimum viable expression of your idea and see if it sells (In hard currency).

But that MVP still takes time and money, and although it raises the confidence that the idea is good, it doesn't guarantee that the end product will sell, that there aren't IP issues standing in the way, that someone else might bring it to market sooner or better, etc. That requires the analyses and projections that Zies (rightfully) introduced to the thread. But those analyses and projections cost time and money too, and again, just raise confidence, don't assure success.

But there is another approach that avoids all that uncertainty - look for PROBLEMS, not ideas. You find problems by talking with others, looking for what's bothering them. And when you find a problem, you don't look for a solution - you encourage others to find a solution - initially those you're talking with, homing in on and defining the problem, and later designing the solution. That may be one or more of the people you're talking with or an outsider brought in with the needed skills. Through this whole process, you're keeping an eye on the costs. bringing them into the discussions as needed to keep the search going to a solution that's viable. Note that you're not creating anything - simply helping others find a solution to what's bothering them - and in the process, if it all comes together, structuring a business for yourself. Every one of my businesses evolved in this way.

Ed Zimmer: Let me illustrate with a real-world example, that of the business I put into my profile. In the '60s, computers were making their way into the auto plants. In the mid-60's, I met one of their QC people, who when he found out that I was selling display technology to the military, asked whether it was feasible to put computer-driven displays along the line so that the QC people could message the assemblers. At the time it wasn't - such displays were far more expensive than they could afford. But, interesting problem - so I started attending local QC meetings and put the word out to my creative network (engineers, scientists, inventors that I had met and stayed in touch with simply because I found the relationships stimulating). Over time we homed in on what was wanted: interface, mounting, visibility, display content, price they needed, etc. About 5 years after initial contact, Intel introduced the MOS shift register and one of my engineer friends instantly recognized that was the answer to the low-cost display problem, designed what the QC people wanted and we set up a business with customers day one.

The coaches/advisers like Zile, would have had a fit with this one. We simply rented a space and started building/shipping. (Many of the local, state and Federal license and tax people even found us before we had time to find them.) There was even a patent claiming the design held by RCA (a Goliath at the time). It was a year before RCA came around to give us a cease-and-desist order, but by that time many of the Goliaths were already designing that display technology into their products so we pleaded, hey we're just a little guy, go after them and if they start paying royalties, so will we. The case went through the courts for the next 16 years and RCA finally lost. (Even if they had won, we'd have been in the clear because after about 10 years they forgot to keep giving us the required annual notice.)

The lesson I'm trying to convey is that business is not nearly as complex as all the pundits here try to make it. All you require to do-business is a customer - and when you have one, JUST DO IT! You'll learn a lot more servicing that customer than you'll ever learn reading books, articles, posts, doing analyses, projections, etc., etc.

Richard Coleness, Andrea, one of the questions you asked was ...is there a quick way to evaluate a business idea. The answer is; yes of course there are quick ways to evaluate an idea ....IF YOU KNOW WHAT THE CORRECT QUESTIONS ARE TO BEGIN WITH....and then believe the answers you are given. I'll bet if there were two people with the same idea, one did a quickie evaluation and the other waited for a variety of inputs the 2nd guy that waits will be more successful.

Ed Zimmer: Richard. The approach I described in my last couple of posts is what resulted in all my businesses and what I currently counsel (and counseled for SCORE with great success until they shut me down a couple of years ago). I'd very much value your opinion of it. What issues do you feel I skimmed over? What problems do you see? Why isn't it used more? And don't mince words as I have a very thick skin.

Zile Soilihi: So , Ed you come up with an interesting point ! Find a problem to solve! Indeed an idea will be successful if it cures a PAIN. This is what value proposition is all about(that brings me back to BM canvas! Sorry Ed for being too structured!!).

Now i would like to come back to the question asked by Andrea ? IS IT A GOOD QUESTION TO ASK ? Why should we answer this question when we're talking business ? Is it SERIOUS to go quickie when you evaluate an idea ? Don't you need to take some time to evaluate an idea before embarking in a journey where you are probably going to spend hours days months and maybe years before profitability ? Your opinion please !

Ed Zimmer: Zile. If you read the example in my last post, you'll see that was 5 years in the making. I always had many of these "problems" in process - some came to a head quickly, some didn't. Some worked out, some didn't. Didn't matter. It was all interesting - all fun - and those that worked out made money (cumulatively, a lot of money). I asked Richard for his critique. I'd like yours too. Ravi's also. Being out of the business mainstream these past few years, I miss the criticism.

Andrea Sica Hi Gentlemen, thank you all for the great answers so far.

Zile, I trust by your experience you understand that "quickly" it's just a way to say. I know that evaluating an idea takes time. I also use the canvas, and I agree with your approach. Although I am also very practical, and I found most of the things that Ed mentioned very helpful. I don't honestly see much conflict among your answers anyway. I just wanted to see whether highly experienced professionals had some kind of "tricks" to share. And I must say that all of you got the real purpose of my question.

Interesting was to have the opinion by some investors as well, as I trust they have a different approach - somehow "quicker" - compared to whom has to turn the idea into a business. So, thank you all so much for sharing your thoughts.

Richard Coleness: Hi Ed, First of all I'm not a critic. As far as I can tell your materials suggested to people have been "on the mark". Personally if I am going to explain things to people I try to keep it short which begs those listening to ask questions, but that is a matter of writing style. The hardest thing I run into is understanding what the real question is...what are they really asking? Sometimes asking a question in return is better than giving an answer.

Just as in Andrea's comment above, he says; "Interesting was to have the opinion by some investors as well, as I trust they have a different approach - somehow "quicker" - compared to whom has to turn the idea into a business." An investor does have a quicker way to evaluate a business, but each investors "trick" to evaluate is different from every other investor. So there is no real correct answer to this observation/question.

The evaluation of a business idea will take as long as a person wishes to accept suggestions or evaluations from others. The question, in reality, should be "How do I know when I have evaluated the idea as far as it needs to be?" or "How do I keep from oversimplifying a business idea?" or "How do I keep from over complicating a business idea."

1. If I was to answer his original question I'd probably just make a list.
2. How big is the market?
3. Is it easy/cheap to make?
4. Can you scale the product quickly?
5. Is there anything similar on the market?

Ed Zimmer: Richard. The purpose of my long posts was to caution Andrea that the instant one takes possession of an idea, one has one strike against them regardless of what they then do. Objectivity gets lost and understanding gets distorted by ego. But, Richard, you're obviously right about keeping responses short as I obviously didn't get that point across.

Tabitha Jean Naylor : In order to successfully evaluate a business idea, you need to spend some time researching and doing some 'hard work' to ensure you have covered all avenues. Sitting down, and putting pen to paper is a great way to evaluate a business idea.

By listing all pros, and cons, you can get a bigger picture look at what is most beneficial and what is not. This will allow you to come to an overall conclusion if this business idea/ venture is truly going to be worthwhile.

A quick evaluation approach is definitely not best. There may be key points you could overlook that would maybe swing the answer of yes it's good, or no it's not worthwhile in a completely different direction if you would have taken time to sit back and look through it properly.

Andrew McWhirter: Spending a few days, or even a few weeks validating your startup idea will help you get a clear approach on how to proceed, and uncover any deal breakers early on. Also, it's a good idea to reach out to your family, friends and colleagues, if you need advice about some of these questions.

Matt Kurleto: Andrew McWhirter, I'm not quite sure about family and friends as a solution. They all want to be supportive which in most cases mean embracing whatever you do. It's much more valuable if your feedback comes from the market. Your dad will give you $50k even without your 10% of equity because he loves you. If you get $50k from a stranger that loves your solution - that's a strong indicator.

Daniel Leping : The tools are great, but some of them are to be used when you have the MVP, not before. Want to add something to the list:

1. Outline what is you business in essence (important for further testing): mission, product, value, position (on the market). These should answer the following questions: why? how? what? for whom?
2. Prerequisite for the experiment. Build your message which consists of at least the mission and the value. Best of all if with the product as well. i.e.:

    - With the strong mindset [mission]
    - Nurtured step by step [product]
    - Get control of your body shape [value]

3. See if there is an audience in your target group (remember position on the market?) which a) believes in your mission b) needs the value you bring. We already have a message we can use for the experiment if there is a traction. It can be tested several ways. One of my favourites is with Facebook ads (cheap and effective for learning).

4. Great metrics ? Start thinking about the experience of the product Otherwise tweak the product, value or position.

" When You Talk, You Are Already Repeating What You Already Know. But If You Listen You May Learn Something New"

---- Dalai Lama

" You Are What You Listen To"

---- Anonymous

Notes That You Should Take

"Answer The Following Set of Questions For Your Business Idea Validation"

- Meet as many people offline and online
- Listen carefully to your target customers
- Find Out How Best You Can Engage With Your Customers ?
- Will Your Customers Pay For The Price Of Your Product/Services?
- Be Flexible To Moderate Your Planning
- Know How Big Is Your Market?
- Know How You Can Scale The Product/Services?
- Primary/Secondary Data Gathering From Your Target Market
- Find People Who Will Love Your Solution
- Build A Strong Value Proposition

" You Become What You Read,
You Become What You Listen To,
You Become What You Watch,
You Become What You Think,
Choose Wisely "

---- Anonymous

" A Brand Is No Longer What We Tell The Customer It Is
It Is What Customers Tell Each Other It Is"

---- Scott Cook

*" Lamborghini's Don't Have Commercials
Because People Who Can Afford Them
Aren't Sitting Around Watching TV"*

---- Joel Osteen

Global Point Of View

As I shared before I also invited some awesome startup specialists, entrepreneurs, mentors, VCs and global experts to share their point of view on the topic. The reason why I took a diverse opinion was to understand the different point of view in the startup ecosystem.

It is imperative for you as a reader to understand that taking an opinion on a subject from experts from various sectors across the globe gives you a perspective from almost all corners that you might have not seen or thought of.

Not all options lead to to success however if we take a diverse view chances of failure gets reduced drastically and with some more focus & knowledge (that you gain from experts) you might as well taste success on the way :)

The objective for assimilating myriad thoughts from across the world is to help you build your business idea in a very clear, crisp and uniform fashion so that whatever startup you are planning to get into, you get a complete perspective of the business idea validation.

You might be a student, homemaker, professional from the corporate world, a budding entrepreneur, someone who has already conceptualized his idea to launch as a business, a retired professional or anyone planning to jump into the chaotic world of startups, there is only one thing that comes always handy to you. **Advices & Lots Of It**.

There is no harm taking advices in fact it is absolutely necessary that the more advices you take from people from across regions, geographies, sectors, levels and functions, the more chances are that you will get a more holistic view for you startup business idea. You will be surprised that some of the suggestions, situations, ideas etc you would have never imagined at all and would have never prepared yourself and your venture for the same.

Stay prepared for the unknown and that's the reason why I always reach out to people, experts to take their opinion to get a different perspective of the same thing that I am thinking.

Keep you notepad and your pen ready to take down notes of each and every new point that you would have not thought about your venture and keep the perspective lighted up with various thoughts and situations.

" Tell Me & I Will Forget,
 Show Me & I May Remember,
Involve Me & I Learn"

---- Benjamin Franklin

Dr Aniruddha Malpani
Investor, Entrepreneur

Many young entrepreneurs have an idea which they feel is very clever and unique, and they want to create a startup in order to bring that dream to reality. However, there is a big difference between having an idea and being able to implement it !

It's easy to get ideas, so how do you decide which idea to pursue ? After all, you do need to focus and set your priorities ! Should you go after the idea which has the highest potential for making tons of money ? Or the one which you are most passionate about ?

How do you decide ?

No amount of mental gymnastics or armchair discussions with friends and family is going to help you move forward - you need to actually get out in the real world and find the answers. The trouble is that most people are just wannabe entrepreneurs - they don't have the courage to actually get out there and execute. They will always find excuses as to why the time is not right , and will always continue dreaming big all their life.

The key question you need to answer is - Will customers pay to use your solution ?

This is the million-dollar question, because ideas are cheap , but being able to execute them well requires a lot of hard work. Young first time entrepreneurs don't really have a good sense of what is involved in running a business, and tend to overestimate their ability to cross all the hurdles which they're likely to face.

This is why you need to share your idea, and discuss it with as many people as possible , so that they can give you feedback . Most people will want to be supportive, because they don't want to dampen your enthusiasm. You need to specifically ask for criticism, otherwise people will tend to sugar coat their true opinion , because they don't want to hurt your feelings. Ask them point-blank - why is this likely to fail ? This may hurt your ego, but you don't want to waste years and lots of money in pursuing a futile idea - this would be much more expensive in the long run !

Many entrepreneurs are jealously possessive about their ideas. They are scared that someone will steal them , and they will lose their "first-mover advantage" They naively believe that no one in the world has ever had such a clever idea before, because they live in their own little bubble , because they have very little real life experience. They usually lack business sense , partly because they are so young, and haven't worked so far.

One way of evaluating the idea is to pitch it to lots of investors and see what they have to say. While investors may not have expertise in your specific domain, they do listen to lots of ideas from lots of entrepreneurs. They will be able to tell you whether your idea is original; what makes it different; and whether it's likely to work or not. However, before you approach an investor, please do your homework , so that you show that you are thoughtful and well-prepared, and understand what's happening in your space.

It's important to have skin in the game, so please spend some of your own money in showing that you have done your best to implement your idea , no matter how limited your funds maybe. Yes, bootstrapping is hard, but this is the definition of an entrepreneur - one who makes do with limited resources ! An investor needs to see that you are willing to work hard, and if he can see that you have done much more than just sit in your chair and create an attractive Microsoft PowerPoint presentation or plot lots of numbers in an Excel spreadsheet, he's much more likely to respect you and give you a patient hearing.

Finally, remember that investors don't have all the answers. They are often wrong, so don't ignore what your gut tells you. The only way to validate an idea is to test it out in the real world . This is the final arbitrator, and until you actually do it, no one really knows whether your idea is going to work or not. Lots of great ideas don't work in real life for multiple reasons - for example, your competition may outclass and outspend you , and there's nothing you can do to reduce this risk of failure. Conversely, what seems to be a terrible idea at first blush can go on to become a wildly successful company, because the founders were willing to slog and pivot as needed.

You need to find the answers for yourself, and this is part of your job description as an entrepreneur. It's scary to have to deal with uncertainty, but the buck stops with you, and you need to have the courage to move on , irrespective of whether you get funding or not. You need to be both irrational and optimistic if you want to succeed.

Whether or not your idea works, I can promise you your journey will be an exciting and interesting one, and you will learn a lot - not only about yourself , but about the real world as well.

Running a startup will teach you far more than an MBA, and will help you become wiser and more mature.

Rajiv Tewari
Entrepreneur, Advisor

Business of business is marketing so it's critical to validate a business idea by testing & retesting the idea before launch. Having worked with several offline and online ventures, I have observed that the absence of test marketing phase accounts for success or failure in most cases. In my view, a start-up entrepreneur should find answers to these 5 key questions to validate a business idea in the pre-launch stage itself:

Is the idea really unique?

Many online start-up entrepreneurs tell me that they have half a million clicks on their site due to their unique sales proposition but the monetization part has many question marks. They are, in effect, confused between the window shoppers and actual buyers. These are clear cases of a mismatch between what the customer is looking for and what is being offered. A test launch with a much smaller sample could have indicated what the customers were looking for.

A simple google check revealed that there were many competitors for the ideas considered to be unique by my start-up clients. Instead of matching the potential buyer's needs, wants and values with the idea, the entrepreneurs were primarily focusing on packaging related uniqueness. Packaging attracted prospects but the lack of unique sales proposition did not result in conversions. In today's world of multiple choices, key differentiation is created by the customer's experience. Satisfied customers bring in more customers and once a venture has a set of satisfied customers then it's easy to communicate their experience to the larger market for gaining market shares. This simply means that the product or service must be experienced by a sample set of target buyers for feedback & corrections before launch. It's like ensuring that a half finished painting is not put for public exhibition.

Is your strategy dynamic enough to adapt to sudden change?

During the dot com bust, in the beginning of this century, many brilliant ideas simply failed as most of the start-up entrepreneurs could not adapt to the unexpected changes. During this period, encouraged with our success at the Indian Express Newspapers in the niche business publications area, I had joined a start-up which was using a similar offline model but had plans to move on to an online interface for e-commerce. We created a world record by launching 30 publications in every possible business publication niche in a period of just six months.

Our venture got a funding of over three times of what was expected but the technology changes did not happen, as projected, and the transit to e-commerce portal soon became a distant dream. Our venture simply sank due to lack of funds. Many of my friends who had left large organizations to join startups during this period met the same fate. Only a handful survived as they had deep pockets. The lesson is that in the start-up phase itself an entrepreneur should build a structure and strategy like an amoeba which is able to adapt to external changes quickly and redirect its resources to ensure survival in the short term and growth in the long term. A good example is that of HCL (Hindustan Computers Limited) where the leadership sold calculators to ensure survival while waiting for the computer market to evolve and grow.

Have I projected and planned strategies based on operating cycles?

An entrepreneur has to keep thinking of opening new avenues of revenue based on leveraging the unutilized capacity of the current venture. This approach has to be built in the thinking and culture of an enterprise at the start up stage itself. Investors usually look at this factor very critically so this is a critical element from the funding point of view too.

While working with a news magazine, our projections indicated that the magazine's circulation would more than double within 3 years. There was no way the advertising rates could be doubled at the same rate so the projections warned us about huge losses in future. This was a very challenging situation as restricting the circulation numbers would have allowed the competitors to gain more readers. The publishing house decided to diversify into Indian Languages by leveraging the same infrastructure on the principles of marginal costing. This opened up new avenues of revenue and cut down the costs of the flagship publication to ensure its profitability at higher circulation figures.

Am I focusing too much on technology?

Only a buyer centric strategy has withstood the test of time so focusing too much on a technology centric strategy can go wrong.

One of the leading agricultural pumps set manufacturing company, with a monopoly position in the market, suddenly began to slide down on market shares. Research findings indicated that the farmers' first preference was for this manufacturer's product but price and maintenance issues had pushed them to the local competitors. Prices of the competitors' products were closer to the loan limits of banks and the additional advantage was that their engines could be repaired by local mechanics. From the technology point of view, the competitors were manufacturing inferior quality slow moving engines; which were heavier to carry; and also consumed far more fuel and electricity.

In contrast, this manufacturer's product could only be repaired by the company's trained personnel, who were located in large towns, and there was usually a waiting period of 15 to 30 days for repairing the engines. The crops would have simply died due to lack of water during such a long waiting period. The prices were double of the bank loan limit though the product was technologically far superior as it consumed less power and could be carried by just two persons from one place to another.

The engineering team almost threw us out of the room on hearing our recommendations in favour of launching low technology products. The market feedback had challenged their entire strategy based on technology leadership. When the market shares dipped further, the manufacturer, finally, agreed to our recommendations and launched a low technology slow moving engine at a low price. The market shares went up again and the commanding position of the brand was restored.

How would the investors evaluate me at each stage of business?

Too much euphoria is created when a start-up venture gets angel funding or an early stage funding. Investment at each stage simply means that the accountability levels get raised for the next level of investors. Start-up entrepreneurs need to keep the investors of all stages in mind right at the time of starting a venture as each investor group invests for its next stage of investors.

Angel funding is usually for proof of concept, yet I have noticed many start-ups quickly investing on a nice office, hiring additional staff and so on. The focus at this stage should be on testing the idea among the customers for its capacity to generate revenues. Chances of getting further funds at each stage would automatically increase if the potential of customer buy in is proved at the angel funding or early stage funding itself.

Rajiv Tewari is the Founder of Marketing & Communication Network On LinkedIn. You can connect with him on rajiv@medianetwork.in

Sandeep Balaji
Entrepreneur, Investor

"Eureka" someone screamed and that doesn't often results in a multi-million dollar business that is sustainable. There are a lot of things that go into making a successful business. I would know especially since I have played this game quite a few times and ended up on the losing side of things on a number of occasions.

Co-Founders

First and foremost thing, which validates your startup, is the willingness of your co-founders to go through the pain with you ☺ There is the huge opportunity that everyone sees but not a lot of them have the guts to jump out of the plane with you. Finding those people who are in it for the right reasons in the first stage of your validation.

Attitude

Your co founders or first set of core employees should be able to throw their weight around, learn quickly and be able to play the janitor or office boys role when required. Most startup are nimble, fast and people who do around 30-70% of the things they have never done in their corporate career or student lives. So Attitude and knowing you have a team with the right attitude is key

Technology

I am of the school of thought that pure technology alone is not a differentiator or a validator of a startup. Yes, maybe inventors and guys like Elon Musk might disagree with me! The applicability of technology (disruption or kaizen) in a specific function or use cases which will help you make more money, save time or reduce effort (Hence less # of people) is the validation.

And as a captain of the startup ship if I have identified a large enough white space for application of my technology (say low cost GPS for the shipping tanker industry) then that's validation. And please bear in mind that I don't need to have the entire tech stack built as of right now.

Receptive Customers

No validation like 3rd party validation from your customers/ prospective customer for a startup. Someone putting money on the table or willing to attach their brand/business to try out your product or service as a reference customer is a big step. After people and culture this is probably the biggest reason startups fail. Making one customer happy means you are onto something and you can "process-ize this " i.e sell to many the same thing with marginal costs and the current customer can refer you to several people.

IP

This is a mixed bag but when a startup has built unique IP, then its validation to an intrinsic value that exists in businesses. Like in any other market - supply and demand and being how relevant determines the validation of the same. I have seen this been wasted in startups and used very effectively for both growth and at exist stage.

Cash Flow

You might have a great team, technology, reference customer, etc but what keeps the light on in the office is the cash flow generated daily and monthly. Investment or Funding is one part of the mix but that in my mind is better deployed to build the product and create a barrier to entry for competition. Hence a validation for a business is revenue/sales that the business generates.

Process

It's a lower requirement of validation for me personally as a startups, but if they have a process or at least understand the areas they can improve upon to become better and leaner, then that helps. Many times you will find companies losing money and also creating delays

Strategic Goals/Timelines/Liquidity Horizon

These are wish lists when it comes to startup validation points. As an entrepreneur or as an investor. But a broad based understanding of the overall 30,000 feet view and milestones to get there is important. It become difficult when you are running a startup full time to be toggling between paying rent and looking at where you would like to be in 3 years.

Joseph Roos
Venture Capitalist, Entrepreneur

Over the course of my 12 year career in private equity and venture capital I have had the benefit of reviewing companies across the business life cycle ranging from pre-revenue startups at launch (e.g. Wink & Nod) to multi-billion dollar businesses founded over 300 years ago (Hudson's Bay Company). As a generalist, I have covered consumer, real estate, technology, entertainment, etc. and participated in all parts of the capital stack from equity to debt. In total, I have analyzed over 5,000 public and private companies at varying stages of growth for investment merit and have designed a thorough due diligence checklist that I will outline below.

TAM - Total Addressable Market

Before allocating any capital to a new business I always look to put the market size into perspective. After determining the size of the market I estimate the penetration rate that can be achieved by a new market entrant over a 12 - 18 month period. In analyzing Wink & Nod we determined that the top 2% of the population accounted for 6.5mm elite households, which equaled a $2B market opportunity. We further estimated that 25% of that demographic buys an average of 2 mattresses every 10 years (135,000 mattress annually), which equates to a $100mm market. Given the success of the online mattress market in the U.S. and the size of the total addressable market in India, Wink & Nod met my stringent market size and penetration rate requirements.

Founding Team & Advisors

From my experience, the team is often more important than the idea as I have experienced plenty of examples of great teams building and iterating a good idea into a great idea. I have not however, seen a mediocre team do the same even if they have a great idea because of their inability to execute. Wink & Nod was founded by several team members with broad and complementary skills sets with backgrounds in private equity, venture capital, investment banking, consulting, technology, and entrepreneurship. Two of the found members had worked together previously on a US based eCommerce business and many of the key learnings with respect to marketing, brand building, social media, finance, legal/structure have been applied to the new venture. I also prefer to invest in founders who have previous entrepreneurial experience and ideally investment exits. The Wink & Nod team is self- funding the business and I have experienced that founding teams with meaningful skin in the game are more committed to the success or failure of the business over the long term. The Wink & Nod team is comprised of an experienced CEO, CFO, and CTO and is supported by industry leading experts in digital marketing, branding, web development, customer service, manufacturing, and logistics.

Product

When looking at a product company I always benchmark the quality, features, and price against the competitive peer set. Product companies can only compete on price, quality, and intangibles (branding, customer service, etc.). As a result of longstanding manufacturing connections in Asia, Wink & Nod is able to leverage deeply negotiated pricing while offering a superior quality product to top consumers in India. The product will meet all of the highest manufacturing standards and will provide a superior sleep experience. Before investing in a consumer product I always use the product personally and share it will my close circle of confidantes. Based on that feedback we engage in channel checks and market research studies to compare the product in question against current market incumbents.

Revenue Visibility & Financial Sophistication

An idea is not a business. Before engaging in further due diligence I require that all founders provide me with at least 3 years of projections, a 12-18 month burn rate projection, and a detailed break-down of the sources and uses of a capital raise. I want founders to treat each dollar with the same scrutiny that I would and be good stewards of investor capital. I want to understand how the founders will use each dollar to ensure that they return more than a dollar on that investment. One of the reasons I like eCommerce business is that it is incredibly easy to measure performance from a digital marketing spend and revenue generated perspective. A business is not viable until revenue streams are identified and customer acquisition costs and channels are well understood. I will only invest in businesses that have at least 18 months of runway to operate a business as I do not want founders to be in perpetual fundraising mode being distracted from operating and growing the business. I look for strong accounting practices and a responsible adult to oversee the finance and accounting department.

Investor Validation

Generally before finalizing an investment I share the deal with a small network of trusted advisors and investors whom I consider to be experts in that particular industry. I am also more inclined to invest in a deal where there is a strong lead investor who has a track record in the specific industry I am investing in. Herd mentality investing is very prevalent in various global investment communities, which can have both positive and negative consequences. My experience has taught me that the positives generally outweigh the negatives as network effects and access to smart investors provides long term value to start-ups.

Avigail Berg-Panitz
Wellness & Social Entrepreneur, Trainer, Advisor

Let's first be on the same page of what is **BUSINESS VALIDATION OF AN IDEA**:

My definition: The process an entrepreneur goes through from the first stage of being intrigued, passionate and interested in an idea/concept/ product/ system, to be convinced himself, and to have the tools to convince clients, partners and investors about its capacity to be a profit generator and a basis for an independent business.

How it started- TheSoundWell www.vibro-therapy.com

Olav Skille (Norway/Finland) The inventor Vibroacoustic Therapy asked me to represent his therapy in America. The first thing that came to my mind was – I want to try Vibroacoustic Therapy on my BodyMind Laboratory to let my cells feel and sense harmonic low sound frequencies and to realize the impact.

My background as life coach and meditation teacher have always made me interested in new therapeutic modalities and self-help tools.

Skille sent me a mat and the frequencies in the range between 30-120hz and started training me over skype, daily.

The bottom line – after treating myself for 3 months – I was convinced – This is what I want to do for the rest of my life!!! Offer Vibroacoustic therapy as B2B and B2C in US and around the world

1. First I needed to be convinced that **THE WHAT is what** you want to do, and that in my perception, Vibroacoustic therapy is the most effective, friendliest and easiest way to reduce mental, emotional and physical stress – daily. Some people can sell ice to Eskimos , for them this may not be a stage in their business validation.

2. **EXPLORE THE MARKET** of Integrative wellness solutions, define its needs, uniqueness and added value, specifically in comparison with companies that may compete with me
3. **CREATE A BUSINESS PLAN** with a business model, evaluation of manufacturing, marketing, sale, evaluation of short term /long term costs. The business plant should have the following:

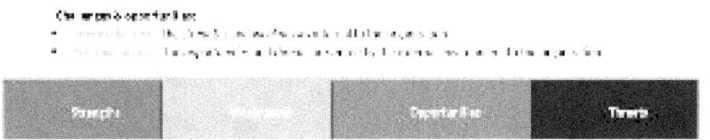

4. **TEAM** –pitching to potential team members and getting feedback from diversified trustful people
5. **EXPLORE COLLABORATION** with potential strategic business partners that complement what I do.
6. **START LEAN** – use Linkedin as alive laboratory to get feedback on the need of your product and start dialoguing with potential b2c and b2b clients
7. **Start sales**
8. Fine tuning business plan on the go
9. Getting ready for three scenarios – angel investment, VC investment, crowdfunding

WHAT QUESTIONS TO ASK YOURSELF IN THE VALIDATION PROCESS ?

      a. WHAT motivates me in this idea and WHY
      b. WHAT are the stages of validation and HOW I define criteria of success
      c. WHAT is the need for my idea
      d. WHAT are the challenges of bringing this idea to the market
      e. WHO do you consult and HOW to I evaluate feedback
      f. How will I find the right team to complete me
      g. WHEN do I start a pilot and WHERE

h. WHAT are the ways to use Linkedin as a business development platform

GOING BACK TO MY OWN CASE STUDY – THESOUNDWELL: I have started to manufacture my own mats and pillows. I have strategic business partners and some business associates. Today more than ever, I'm convinced I'm on the right track with having Vibroacoustic Therapy as the best, most effective and easiest way to reduce mental, physical and emotional stress daily. Though I fined tuned my business plan more than once – I know that will persistence, flexibility and creativity, Vibroacoustic Therapy will be used by therapists and health practitioners as an added value modality and by direct clients as a self-help tool to activate 6P wellness: preventive, proactive, personalized, positive persevering wellness-wellbeing platform .

Edward Frankel
Serial Entrepreneur, Corporate Coach, Advisor

When creating a new enterprise, one should analysis not only the specific segment of the economic environment. Other important areas of observation are imperative, let's review:

1) Who is in the segment you wish to pursue;
2) Are there differentiates already operating in this space;
3) What are people saying about the space;
4) Do you have a clear-cut avenue to differentiating yourself from others?

The above is a short list, however, one can expand the list to flesh out other problem areas to solve and use as a sounding board for your team.

I started with the four questions since most startups are evolved from one person's ideas, that is not to say teams of like minded people friends and associates sometimes create companies.

So, once you address these four questions and others you are ready to go to the next step. The next step is how to put your dream team together? Obviously, a team leader should have so choice candidates in mind. Remember best friends often turn out not to be the best choices, why "familiarity often breeds contempt"

Choose team members based upon their prior work experience and knowledge, also more importantly are they team players and can they take direction in a positive manner.

As a serial entrepreneur, I always have tried to bring to the team people with leadership skills above my own, yes you must subordinate your ego even at times you know you can do a better job. The key is knowing all new companies will go through growing pains and at times the company may face failure. Growing from these setbacks makes a company stronger, be it missing launching a product or a platform. A stronger leadership will emerge from what has occurred. To that point, it is conceivable that you observe a junior member of the team that steps up and takes the lead in correcting direction with new leadership. In cases if that does not happen you may have to take the reins or bring someone with the right skills to the party.

Other considerations are required in forming a new enterprise

Question number one is how do you fund your new business?
I am going to dismiss the known sources of capital at this juncture since you all have been exposed to the gospel of funding a venture backed or angel and friends and family component. What are your objectives comes first, yes what is it that you want from building this company?

Many people overlook this part of your sacrificing a good part of your life to accomplish. We are addressing the goal of building a new company, remember not all people are Steve Jobs, Bill Gates or Mark Zuckerberg. We all can't become billionaires; a good life requires some down time for enjoyment. Balance is a key component of having what is right for you.

So again, the first thing you must do is set a path for your lifestyle, does that mean you delay getting married and not having children until you are in your late forties or finding the equiLibrium to do both. It is your choice and direction when pursuing a new venture.

The next step and most will tell you secure your funding first, while I will tell you gather talent and resources to prove your concept before you go to the name funding sources. Why because it will enable you to have a much better negotiating chip and save you from giving up control of your business and the equity you deserve.

You can get in touch with Ed on edf07@comcast.net

Diana Palchik
Trademark and Business Lawyer, Legal Specialist

Did you know that the holder of a patent for the fidget spinner lost rights to her invention simply because she didn't file patent renewal documents that would have cost several hundred dollars? While fidget spinner sales generate millions of dollars for other companies, the toy's inventor is struggling financially and trying to make ends meet.

A business idea's successful implementation will often depend on some form of intellectual property. A highly marketable brand name or unique website design can be valuable IP. A novel invention may be a startup's main competitive advantage.

1. Do you know what IP you have?
2. Are you certain that it's yours?
3. Can you readily obtain IP that you still need?
4. You'll need to have satisfactory answers to these types of questions so that the IP underpinning your business idea is on solid footing.

If your idea is based on existing intellectual property, such as a patented invention of one of your founders, you'll need to find out whether the patent documentation is up to date. To avoid the fidget spinner outcome, you'll have to make sure you have exclusive rights to exploit the invention behind your business plan.

You'll need to find out whether the IP that's relevant to your business idea is already tied up by someone else. Is the invention you want to market actually owned by your employer, or even your competitor? Does your graphic designer really own your website because there's no contract in place, or the contract isn't clear?

Before choosing a name, logo, or tagline, you should conduct a proper trademark availability search to determine whether someone has already taken that branding. Doing an internet search and finding no exact hits does not mean the coast is clear. It means you need to dig deeper. Trademark searching can be tricky. You'll need to search the national trademark registry, state trademark registries, and possibly international trademark registries. You will have to evaluate similar names, not just identical ones. The legal test is whether confusion is likely to result. That means you should check for variations, sound-alikes, and look-alikes.

The trademark registration process normally takes six months to one year if there are no significant issues with the application. The ideal time to apply for a trademark is right after you get a clean availability search result, and sometimes even before. It's a race. In the U.S., the first one to file an application, even for a mark that's not being used, can get priority over the first user of the mark.

Consider your long term goals at the beginning. Registered trademarks are more valuable than unregistered trademarks—to investors and to prospective purchasers of your startup. In an acquisition scenario, valuation of your IP portfolio will be conducted, and a value assigned to each of your intangible assets. The "chain of title" will be traced. Due diligence in the early days of your business venture will help ensure smoother sailing later.

Diana Palchik is a trademark and business lawyer who has worked at several Fortune 500 companies. She currently advises small and medium-sized businesses on trademarks and deal strategies and assists beauty, health, and wellness businesses through her trademark service, Beauty Mark. You can email her at diana@lo-dp.com

Patrick Osman
Entrepreneur, Sales Guru

Throughout the next couple of pages, I will explain how to validate your startup business idea and how to implement it as well as crush the market with your idea in 6 simple steps.

Step 1 – Belief

If you don't genuinely believe in what it is that you are doing, there is no way that your business idea can succeed. According to the oxford dictionary, the term belief is defined as; 'an acceptance that something exists or is true, especially one without proof'.

The importance of having belief in your startup idea is that it will reinforce your confidence throughout the times when the market won't accept your offer, which will then be a shield of defense towards your self doubt.

Belief in your startup idea will overthrow any form of external influenced self-doubt. Self-doubt isn't something that comes with the initial thinking of the idea phase, its something that comes later on, once the market starts to reject what it is that you offer. Understand that specific market segments will reject what you have to offer but you need to persevere throughout the nonsense and rely on your belief, to then satisfy the market segment that needs your services, because they are out there.

Step 2 – Solution to a current problem?

When I started the sales training academy about 1 year ago, (www.salestrainingacademy.online) it was because I noticed one thing. What I noticed was that there are so many startup companies out there who are struggling to sell their product and the reason why is because they are not providing a solution to a current problem.

A lot of companies out there in this generation, are struggling to generate new business because their products are not being sold the way they should be. Throughout the corporate world, products are not being pitched properly and psychology is not something that is being heavily focused on when it comes to training. Therefore I created the sales training academy, which is an online sales course that trains individuals in *any* industry how to sell any product psychologically. Whether it be a product or service priced at $3.00 or a product or service at $1,000,000.

Whatever product or service it is that you're looking at entering the current market place with, make sure that the output is a solution to the current markets problem. Once you release a product or a startup idea, the markets response will be based on your output and how effective your product/service can be.

Step 3 – Perspectives from people who have done it before

With any idea that comes to your mind, allow it to process. Don't immediately cancel it out and think that it will not work. If it is a business idea in which you have not worked in or a field that you do not have expertise in that specific area listen and do not be quick to judge. What you need to do is really simple, do not seek perspectives of people who have not done it before, seek the perspectives of individuals in that specific area, experts in that specific field/industry or someone who has done it before.

What a lot of entrepreneurs do in the early stages is seek the wrong perspectives i.e. their friends, family or other people that are not considered the correct credible and reliable to source information from. 9 Out of 10 times, those individuals will give you the wrong advice because they don't know that industry accurately enough to give you the correct feedback. When you seek the perspectives of individuals who have done it before, they will show you the upsides and downsides as well as explain the challenges you will face as they would have faced them in the past, which will then lead to them explaining how they overcame those specific challenges.

Step 4 – Develop a plan

I want you to picture two boats in a large ocean. (Boat A) One boat has a captain, full boat crew and a specific destination in place. (Boat B) The other boat is plain empty, does not have anyone in the ship. What do you think is going to happen? Boat A is going to arrive at its destination because it has a captain steering it in the right direction, whilst the water will take Boat B to wherever the direction of the current is flowing. Don't be Boat B, be Boat A.

Have a direction and develop a specific plan as to how you're going to achieve whatever it is that you want to achieve. It needs to be a specific step by step plan that documents your what's, why's and most importantly your how's. This will further reinforce your confidence in your idea and this will always give you something to work on, on a daily basis, as you will be forced to work towards your specific goal and your plan will dictate how you're going to achieve reaching your goal.

Step 5 – Stay Committed

If you are not committed, you may as well throw in the white towel now. Commitment is key in any business, when it comes to you starting a business, you need to put your blood, sweat and tears into it. At the end of every tunnel there is a light, but most people back out of an early start up because they are influenced by what they see in that tunnel, which is pure darkness. You need to keep freaking working, you are going to see the light, it is going to happen, I remember when I first was recording all my videos and finally released the sales training academy, there were so many times where I said to myself, this is not going to succeed, all this self doubt was hitting me, but I did not allow anything to come between me and my goal because number 1, I had solid belief in my product and number 2 I stayed committed. Once I released it, I now have start up businesses all around the world working alongside me, doing the sales training course and increasing sales revenue in their business, strictly because I did not listen to my self doubt and I stayed committed. NOTHING can stop you.

Step 6 – Think Big

Always think big, never think small. Albert Einstein once said 'logic can take you from A to B but imagination will take you to places in which you have never been before'. In my book 'Your Life Your Business' I wrote, "Don't be influenced by your surroundings, but be influenced by your imagination". Always remember that you are one human out of 7 Billion on this planet, stop and think about that number. Billion, now times that by 7.

You are ONE, there are so many people out there that are busting for your services, so don't think about servicing the people within your city or your province, but be willing to service people on the other side of the planet! The internet has made international business so easy to do now, you can generate a sale from your phone in your bed at 4 am! In 1937, Nikola Tesla said "when wireless is perfectly applied the whole earth will be converted into a huge brain, which in fact is, all things being particles of a real and rhythmic whole. We shall be able to communicate with one another instantly, irrespective of distance. Not only this, but through television and telephony we shall see and hear one another as perfectly as though we were face to face, despite intervening distances of thousands of miles; and the instruments through which we shall be able to do this, will be amazingly simple compared to our present telephone. A man will be able to carry one in his vest pocket. My fellow entrepreneurial friend, that day is here. Get up, change the world and constantly do big things.

Feel free to contact Patrick directly about your business ventures at (Patrick@patrickosman.com) and if you need any assistance with your sales performance, go and learn the psychology behind persuasion at www.salestrainingacademy.online

Pranab Sen
Entrepreneur, Consultant

"Startups fail not because they can't create products or services; they fail because they can't find customers for those products or services......
Steve Blank

It is evident from various startup ecosystems that 90% of the startups fail to take-off and sustain due to lack of differentiated value offering and poor unit economics. Before launching a product or service to the market, it is imperative to evaluate the Product-Market fit, that helps in validating your business idea. As Harvard Professor Michael J Skok states, the perfect storm happens when **Disruptive business model, Discontinuous innovation and Underserved market** overlap.

Startups need to Create, Deliver and Capture Value to gain a competitive advantage and penetrate the market, not just for innovators and early adopters, but for majority of the target market. Building a unique value proposition plays a major role in the process of business model validation, where startup entrepreneurs must communicate how they are solving the customer problem in a differentiated manner, to the target market.

At ResearchFox Consulting, the firm I cofounded, we have helped venture capital firms, accelerators and startups in providing a plethora of solutions. Over our half-a-decade of working in the startup ecosystem, we have been propagating the message that, before launching a solution in the market, startups must validate their business model, run Proof of Concept (PoC), product feature and user acceptance testing, and chart a robust Go to Market (GTM) strategy, to succeed in the competitive market.

Business model validation is non-negotiable as it validates assumptions, and successful startups do it better before launching their solution in the market. Below are the 3 key parameters while validating your business idea:

- Customer Need & Product-Market Fit
- Existing Market Offerings, Competition & Gap
- Sustained Value Creation and Strong Unit Economics

Of the above three, Customer need identification is a vital step to validate your business idea. This should be an in-depth qualitative research where you get to know the below insight about the customer and your solution:

- Do they have a real problem/need?
- Are they looking for a Solution?
- Where does your Solution stand compare to competitors?
- Will they Pay the Price?
- What are the influencers or drivers for Purchase
- Will they buy with your Product's Features?

The above questions can be answered by carrying out a market research through various methods like:
1. Participatory Design and Evaluation (Illustrations, Storyboards, Buyer Persona, Feature Testing),
2. Lab studies (Prototype Evaluation, Customer behaviour)
3. Indirect Observation (Mock Sales, Tracking actions)

It is as important to decode the customer needs, as to finding out whether your solution is the right fit for them. Customer's always look for ways to get over their pain points and don't care about the type of solution you offer. Startup which can decipher the customer's need better and develop differentiated and strong value proposition, etch a strong presence in the market. Uber was successful disrupting the ride-hailing space, because they tapped the app economy for creating a better mobility experience, for moving from Point a Point B, by deciphering that people wanted cost-effective, hassle-free, rapid and ubiquitous mobility.

Startup need to consider 3 dimensions of Customer, Marker and Operation for idea vetting

For Customer dimension, it is important to evaluate 3 Key Parameters:

- Value Perceived - Is your Product a Must-have or Nice to have for the Customer?
- Purchase Propensity - Will Customer spend effort and money in buying your product?
- Choice - What are the substitutes or alternatives in market for the customer?

For Market dimension, it is important to evaluate 3 key parameters:

- Who are your competitors in the market and what is their differentiation or positioning?
- What are the gaps in the existing market offerings?
- What are possible entry barriers and drivers for your solution?

For Operations dimension, it is important to evaluate 3 key parameters:

- How you will reach the customers in a cost-effective way to deliver your solution. Is your Customer Acquisition Cost (CAC), which is a factor of sales and marketing cost and the number of customers, best in the market?
- How will you engage and retain them for creating a greater Lifetime Value (LTV)? LTV should always be 3x greater than CAC.
- How can you upsell your services and deliver more value to them in long term?

Top 5 Reasons for Start-up Failure

- Failure in finding the must-have product rather than nice to have products (Product-Market Fit)
- Weak barrier to entry (clones and me-too product / service)

- Challenges in acquiring customers or Customer Acquisition Cost is greater than the Lifetime Value (CAC > LTV)
- Poor Execution of the Team
- High cash burn rate and weak unit economics

Pranab Sen is the Co-Founder of ResearchFox Consulting Pvt. Ltd.

Tishana Simon
Research Specialist and Expert

I love animation movies. To me, it's reality but with a clay form finish and a quick life lesson thrown in. One of my favorite movies from my late teens was Robots. In the story, a young robot named Rodney invents a helper machine called Wonderbot. To create Wonderbot, after many failed inventions, Rodney does intensive technical research. Following a series of adventurous meetings and mishaps, he becomes the Vice President of a big robotic company.

Back then, even before I entered my current field, I wondered "He still had Wonderbot! Will it be a demanded by the citizens of Robot City?" With all the research Rodney did, he never questioned if it will be needed by the functioning robots or if something similar was already made and getting into production. He never validated his product or idea.

In the story Rodney's inspiration, Mr. Bigweld of the robotic company Bigweld Industries noted:

"You know, I love to tinker, but all the tinkering in the world isn't useful unless it starts off with a good idea. So, look around for a need and start coming up with ideas to fill that need. One idea will lead to another, and before you know it... [knocks over a domino row which leads to the last one flipping a light on] ...you've done it! See a need, fill a need!"

But all the ideas in the universe, no matter how great or useful, is not worth the time you took to think it up, if you don't validate through research.

As a business researcher in the Caribbean, I have had clients approach me questioning their way forward. Because of confidentiality, I cannot elaborate, but, for example, one of my clients at the end of the research validation was glad she took the step to contact my company as it saved her money, time and exertion.

So how do we validate your startup business ideas through research?

Validate Through Reports

Depending on the country you live in, market reports are available aplenty. The Euromonitor International gives you free reports on product and service markets. Even check your local Central Statistical offices for their reports. In my country, Trinidad and Tobago, a farmer, for example, can use past reports on agriculture to assess which crop is the most produced.

In the Caribbean or lesser developing countries, however, market reports for purchase may not be available. Crafty thinking may be important here. If you know someone who works at potential your competitor, ask to see his/her company's reports. Unfortunately, these reports most times hide the bad news. So, also enquire if they know if the company has any ideas along the lines of what you have. Please do not give too much detail, the last thing you need is for your idea to be stolen. Because you are taking a risk with your idea, however, you may be reluctant to take this approach. So other validation options are more possible.

Validate Through Databases/Central Statistical Office Websites

Data is available everywhere on the net and in libraries. It just takes the effort to look. If you're in Canada for example, the Canadian Industry Statistics (CIS) can let you know so much about you industry. So let's say, you have an idea for a new Dance Academy that has a potential unique selling point. You aren't too sure if the idea already exists. You're not too sure how many competitors you may have, or what is the going rate if you do get employees. All of these queries are answered in the database of the CIS.

For idea makers in data deficient developing countries, I encourage you again to use what you've got. Though data may not be as extensive or as detailed as Canada or the United States of America, creative thought may be applied. For example, the Economic Commission for Latin America and the Caribbean has an interface with indicators for different sectors.

So, if you want to open up your own tour company and would like to know potential international demand, there is the "Inbound tourism arrivals" variable. Depending on what you found for your country, you may scrap your whole idea (or not).

Validate Through People

Sometimes you want to know what people would think about your idea. *Surveys* are a great way to assess your vision.

Draft up a really short and clear questionnaire.

Really think about what you want to know from others with respect to the idea.

1. What cost would they be willing to pay?
2. At what scale from "Bad" to "Great" do they think of this idea?
3. Where do they shop for goods similar to yours?

After you create your questionnaire head out to where the people who will care about your product or service may be.

1. Have a new idea for a retail store? Head out to the mall.
2. Want to know what tourists think? Commute to tourist hot spots in your country.
3. Want to know what fruits locals buy the most? Visit your local market.

Ask questions and you will get answers that may shock you.

Validate Through Google

So we talked about databases and reports being a method of idea validation through research. You may realize by now that you have to use some sort of search engine to access these. Google, Firefox, Internet Explorer or whatever your preferred engine is your buddy in validation. Not only do reports and databases validate ideas but forums, archived online newspapers, blogs, anything that can give you a hint as to the thoughts of the market.

Conclusion

Sure at the end of the movie, Rodney is successful, but it would have been great to know if Wonderbot was profitable. Don't keep your idea in question (like the movie). Use research to validate whatever concept that is driving your passion.

You may find that with the search comes a new idea, new tweaks to your product or service that will make it highly demanded, or you may just save your investments and efforts by not going forward. In any case, it's better than blindly guessing and hoping for success.

With a Master's degree in Economics, Tishana Simon has extensive knowledge in the elements of research, data analysis, and document editing. Tishana's know-how has spanned socio-economic development issues, health economics, market research and research for government institutions. She can be reached on http://dmresearchtt.com/

THE GIST: Global Point Of View

Here is the Gist from the ideas of the Global Experts:

Joseph, Venture Capitalist, Entrepreneur
You need to know the following:

1. Total Addressable Market (TAM)
2. Founding Team & Advisors
3. Your Product Offering
4. Revenue Visibility & Financial Sophistication
5. Investor Validation Of Your Product

Avigail, Life Coach, Entrepreneur
You should have the following:

1. Clarity
2. Explore the Market
3. Business Plan
4. Team
5. Explore Collaboration
6. Start Lean
7. Start Sales Early
8. Answer All These Questions Regarding your Business:- How, When, What, How

Edward Frankel, Corporate Coach, Advisor
You need to know the following:

1. Who is the target segment you wish to pursue ?
2. Who all are operating in the space you wish to come in ?
3. What are people talking about the space you want to operate in ?
4. Do you have a USP for your business ?

Diana, Trademark & Business Lawyer
You need to know the following:

1. Do you know if you need an IP for your product and service ?
2. Consult a legal expert early
3. Conduct a Legal Search to validate the usage of your product/services
4. Save time and Save money by investing into your legal advice

Dr Aniruddha Malpani, Investor, Entrepreneur
You need to know the following:

1. Will customers pay for your product and services ? Find Out
2. Accept Criticism in the business validation process
3. Pitch to as many investors as possible, Get Feedbacks
4. Bootstrap first and initiate your business
5. Test, Deploy, Test, Deploy, Keep repeating

Rajiv Tewari, Founder, Entrepreneur
You need to know the following :

1. Is your idea unique ?
2. Is your strategy dynamic ?
3. Have you planned strategies based on operating cycles ?
4. Are you focussing too much on technology rather than business ?
5. Think of how investors will evaluate you at every stage of business

Sandeep Balaji, Entrepreneur, Investor
You need a basic business validation through the following :

1. Co Founders discussion
2. The Right Attitude
3. Technology Validation
4. Receptive Customers
5. Intellectual Property

6. Understanding of Cash Flows
7. Process and Controls
8. Strategic Goals and Liquidity Understanding

Patrick Osman, Entrepreneur, Coach, Advisor
You need to have the following:

1. Self Belief
2. Solution to a current problem
3. Perspective from people who have done this type of business before
4. Develop a robust plan
5. Stay committed to business
6. Think BIG

Pranab Sen, Entrepreneur, Business Consultant
You need to validate the following:

1. Customer Needs and Product Market Fit
2. Existing Market Offerings, Competition & Gaps
3. Sustained Value Creation & Strong Unit Economics

Tishana Simon, Research Expert, Entrepreneur
You need to validate your business with the following :

1. Validation Through Existing Reports
2. Validation Through Databases
3. Validation Through People
4. Validation Through Google and Internet

" Meet More People Than Surfing The Internet "

---- Me

*" Never Say Never, Because Limits
Like Fears, Are Often An Illusion "*

---- Michael Jordon

" The Only Source Of Knowledge Is Experience "

---- Albert Einstein

*" When Something Is Important Enough
You Do It Even If The Odds
Aren't In Your Favour "*

---- Elon Musk

The Final Revision

After going through all the details and thoughts on how you need to validate a business idea, here is the synopsis of the whole process which can give you a crux of the whole matter in your business validation process.

Some more useful facts & tips to validate your business idea in a nutshell:

1. **Don't Overlook The Following During Your Business Validation Process:**
    a. Don't overlook the business basics
    b. Don't overlook similar startup experiences in your region and globally
    c. Take stable advices from mentors, advisors, investors, peers
    d. Don't rush into getting things done faster
    e. Don't get misguided with your heart
    f. Don't overlook readily available data in the similar space.
    g. Get some primary or secondary data into perspective to validate the business
    h. Don't ONLY look at money but work on the business process
2. " **Ideally**" your startup business idea should be from any of these 5 buckets :
    a. It is currently solving a real world problem
    b. It is aiming to bridge an existing gap in the market
    c. You plan to build economies of scale
    d. You plan to create a new market altogether (disrupt/innovation)
    e. There is a NEED for your product i.e. There is an addressable market/customers (large) for your product/services
3. **"Prefer" To Work On Your Areas Of Interest or your Hobbies:** or something you might love doing. Time and again people want to do something to follow other people and sometimes they lose interest in

the whole process. This ideally this could come out of the following buckets:
   a. Your current hobbies
   b. Things that you would want to do
   c. Things that you think you are good at
   d. Things that match with your learnings and education
   e. Things that inspire you
4. **Insource Your Ability Areas and Outsource Your Weakness Areas** : This means if you are good at tech and coding keep the tech work with you in validation stage and build your POC/MVP however if you need to get some marketing done to either look for a co founder or a team which is good in marketing your products/services. You can always learn and understand things but it takes its own sweet time to do but it is highly recommended that you outsource critical functions that are not your strength areas or let's say your weak areas. This works great all the time right from the validation stage onwards as you should have your own SWOT Matrix (Strength , Weakness, Opportunities, Threat) ready
5. **Answer these questions Who, Why, When, How, What, Where VERY clearly**
6. Write them down in detail if you want. This will become part of your business plan and/or will clearly help you in answering queries if you are also planning to raise funds. These pointers will also help you crease out lot of your business validation queries.
   a. **Who** is my Target Audience (TA) for my product or services ?
      i. Have I identified and spoken to them or is there a PTP (Promise to pay) for my product/services ?
      ii. Do I have a ready addressable market ?
      iii. Do I have some paying customers in my kitty ?
      iv. Will they agree to pay for my product or services if I approach them ?
      v. Have i made a list of these prospects ?
      vi. Have I made a plan to outreach my TA ?

vii. What will be my outreach mechanisms ? e.g. Content Marketing, Inbound Marketing , Direct Calling etc
b. **Why** would my TA need my product/services ?
   i. Is there a need/gap/new market/economies of scale ?
   ii. Is there some primary and secondary validation that I have taken ?
   iii. Why would the Target Audience buy your product ?
c. **When** am I planning to launch and sell ?
   i. Have you defined the timelines and worked on it ?
   ii. Does it makes senses with respect to the Target Audience ?
   iii. Is that the right time of the year right to launch ? e.g. You are planning to start a digital marketing company...Generally the budgets of the companies are freezed in March or December so ideally you should start a month or two before this so that you can build your sales pipelines.
d. **How** do you plan to market and sell your product/service ?
   i. How Do you plan to build operations for business ?
   ii. Have you done your homework ?
   iii. How are you planning the various functions of the company
      1. E.g. For your marketing channel , Would you use Direct marketing, Channel marketing, digital marketing etc ?
      2. E.g. For sales are you looking at direct sales or online sales ?
e. **What** are you EXACTLY selling ?
   i. Have you defined your USP (Unique Selling Proposition) ?
   ii. Is there really one USP ? e.g. Are you selling a remedy to an existing problem or are you planning to create a new market altogether ?

        iii. This will define your GTM (Go To Market) Planning before in hand
        iv. What is the kind of pricing ? Have you validated that ?
        v. What is the kind of ROI you are expecting ? e.g. Have you validated with competition ?
        vi. What will be your Burn Rate ? (Monthly operational expenses in total say per month e.g. the total burn rate for my startup is expected to be around 20,000 USD)
        vii. What are the kind of revenues you are projecting ?
        viii. When are you planning to get the operational breakeven ?
    f. **Where** are you selling your products/services ? **Where** Will Funds Come From ?
        i. e.g. are you doing it offline, online ? Which is better ?
        ii. Have you worked and iterated on this ?
        iii. Where is your TA located ? Have you validated this ?
        iv. How am I funding my costs ? Where are the funds coming ?
        v. Do I have funds till the time i get **Breakeven** ?

7. Addendum to point no 1 is " **Have a valid, relevant and latest data** " with you for building your projections for each of the points mentioned below. This could be both primary and secondary data. Let's take an example of say building a business for ebooks for Abacus.

    E.g. Who is my TA for selling e-books for Abacus ?
    a. Is it for junior section students from class 1 to class 5 ?
    b. Is it teachers who would be teaching those students ?
    c. Is it parents ?
    d. Now when i have identified e.g. this ebook is targeted at all the above, then I need to have some relevant data in terms of **WHERE** I need to sell. So lets say i need to sell this ebook in New Delhi, Mumbai and Singapore.
    e. Then i need to decide **HOW** e.g. Offline or Online or Franchise or Channel partners

f. How is my competition doing it ?
g. How is the TA responding to the current demand in the market ?
h. For all the above if I have some secondary data and some first point primary data I can **MOST LIKELY** validate my business planning.

8. **No Shortcuts To Success** - Take the long way for doing this with no shortcuts. Real evaluation: First, define who would buy what you're thinking of. Then, if B2C or B2B, find a way of meeting them - in-person (conferences, trade shows, cold calling, etc.). If B2C, primary source are manufacturers, distributors, retailers selling to your prospects, and meet them the same way. Good approach, "I'm thinking about doing such-and-such. What do you think?". And LISTEN. You'll soon know whether the idea is worth pursuing - and if it is, you'll gain a whole new light on what it is you need to pursue.

9. **"Try the Business Model Canvas approach"** which is efficient even you don't have a business model yet. It helps you, ask the questions.. E.g.
    a. What is my "idea" value proposition ?
    b. Who are my customers ?
    c. How will i engage with them ?
    d. How would i generate money ?
    e. What are the channels I would use ?
    f. Who would be my key partners ?
    g. What will be my key cost and revenue streams ?

You can download a clear version of Business Model Canvas: By Business Model Alchemist - http://www.businessmodelalchemist.com/tools, CC BY-SA 1.0

10. **Build A Product Life Cycle Board (PLCB):** If you are planning to launch a product than this PLCB might be useful to you for the following things :
    a. Building matrix for the idea
    b. How to gather the right and relevant data for your product/market ?
    c. What will be your strategy for product roll out and business case ?

d. What will be your Go To Market planning ?
e. How will you build, deploy & test and take feedbacks from early adopters ?
f. How to plan your growth ?

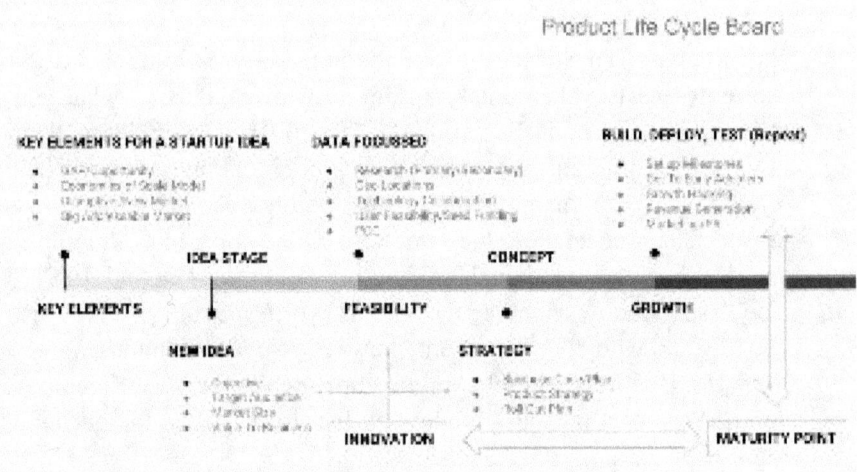

11. **Forget spreadsheets**, if you don't like them , forget BM canvas if you don't like it ! But at the end of the day you need to put figures somewhere, you need some data to bring your idea to the market. Keep your data ready.
12. **When you have your customers are working with you**, there's no need for deep evaluation, iterations and structuring. Have your customers test your prototype and give you feedback, time and again to improve your product and services. This is best shortcut, Go lean, go to your customers first :)
13. **Building a Prototype & MVP (Minimum Viable Product)** and testing with the close knit customers you may have and get the product tested and build it up.
    a. Then you can later reach the markets at large and plan your GTM (Go to market) planning.

       b. How fast you can build your prototype and take it to your customers to test the product is the key.
       c. Once the POC (Proof Of Concept) Is validated you can build your MVP and take it back to the Target Audience/Customers and start refining your product.
       d. Go Early, Go Lean, Go Fast, Keep improving. Don't wait for perfection.
14. **Hire a Mentor or Advisor** : It is Priceless to have a mentor/advisor on board from the early stages of the business idea validation.
       a. He or she not only helps you in handholding through the process,
       b. He or she critically looks at the idea and feasibility at all steps with you.
       c. Without looking here and there it is one thing that you should look at from the inception stage itself
15. **Don't EVER Rush** : There is absolutely no need to rush into your business till you have done the groundwork completely. All opportunities and possibilities can wait. The money won't fly away, the business will not fly away. First you need to valid your idea and once you have done that get into your business or go ahead sign some documents.
16. **Trust Diligently** : Do not blindly trust ANYONE before you have done the validation of your business idea completely.
       a. Post that you can go ahead and discuss details with your co founders or your partners.
       b. If you feel otherwise and have rightful questions, go ahead ask them and you need answers for the same.
       c. Do not sit quiet till all your queries whether spoken or unspoken have been answered completely.
       d. Ask questions, it's better to be foolish in the start when you are in the inquisitive stage then be doomed in the end with million questions unanswered
17. **Hiring Teams** : Do not hire any teams or employees till the time you have not validated your business idea and done some due diligence on

the business. This is the single most biggest mistake that anyone can do, you are basically risking not only business but some careers as well with this. Keep in mind the structuring of the business can be done well and fast once you have validated your business and you have a strong product (Tested in the right Target Audience)

18. **Choosing the right Co-Founder**: Once you have validated your business idea and structured the entire business planning in your head should you discuss the idea of bringing some 'Reliable' co-founder on board if required. You would by now know why and what will a co-founder do in the business as you have structured the entire business and validated it with your data. You would be clear in your Go To market planning. Having a Co-Founder is not an absolute necessity however:
    a. If there is a possible synergy for business , you can explore this option and on board one.
    b. If you do not have the required skills in your validated business model then you should look at like minded people
    c. Keep ethics and integrity as the top elements to screen
    d. Prefer having a Co-Founders agreement to avoid any hassles in the future even if you are working with you best friends or family

19. **Human Capital :** This is the most important thing that you should understand at the validation stage. Howsoever powerful or disruptive your business idea might be but if you don't have the right human capital (beyond the co-founders) you are asking for serious trouble. Let me simply for you. Now if you have validated your business idea potential, here is what is important for you to know which of these three you are falling ino:
    a. A great team with a validated business idea
    b. A non competent team with a great validated idea
    c. A great team with a validated idea

You can afford to be in buckets a & c but never in the bucket b. You are asking for trouble if you fall in bucket b.

20. **Legal Documentation**: Do not get into any agreements, documentation or collaboration in a legal format till the time you have done your primary and secondary homework on your business idea validation and you are sure you are going in a certain direction.
    a. E.g. you want to start a mobile app for parents to locate their kids in the daycare on what they are doing at a certain point of time.
    b. Don't rush into building legal agreements with schools, vendors etc
    c. Once you have validated all of the who, where, why, when, how of the business idea then only get on to building a LLP or LLC for your venture or say plan and hire human capital.
    d. Point c will give you the scope of work and the legal agreements that you might want to work with
    e. Check the requirement for Intellectual Property for your product or services
    f. Consult a lawyer or legal specialist for various things like trademark, IP, patents etc which might be used for your product or services
21. **Talk To Existing Entrepreneurs** : That's the best thing you can invest in. Talking to entrepreneurs especially the ones who have been on the same road and time and again done the same thing over and over again. They might share their point of view on the following things :
    a. Talk to entrepreneurs Regionally & Globally, you might find different and varied perspectives
    b. Reach out to as many entrepreneurs as you can and do it constantly...Entrepreneurs are busy people, you will eventually also get busy so keep reaching out to them time and again. Ensure you reach out to many entrepreneurs, only few might revert so that's fine but keep the dialogue open and on a larger perspective. Don't give up on this.
    c. Ask them: What to do and What not to do ?
    d. Ask them: How to approach the business ?

- e. Ask them: How to plan for growth ?
- f. Ask them: What kind of costs and revenues you might have ?
- g. Ask them: What kind of challenges you might face in the market ?
- h. Ask them: What kind of human capital you might need for the business ?
- i. Ask them: When should you ideally start your business ?
- j. Ask them: How to build a good startup culture ?
- k. Ask them: How to hire a good team ?
- l. Ask them: How to start your business with what you already have ?
- m. Ask them: How to get data and what kind of data might be required to validate your business idea ?

22. **Ability :** You should for sure know this and answer. If you can't then you should ask your mentor or your advisor to help you out. The question is simple to ask yourself " **Do I have the ability to lead and execute this business that I am about to start ?** " If the answer is Yes from all sides, its fair BUT if the answer is a big fat NO then you need to seriously think about it . Do not jump into ANY business whether lucrative or not if :
    - a. You do not have the right technical expertise to run the business. This means is either you should know about how the business will happen or you should have the right human capital who can help you in building the business. This is because the dependability on the business will be huge on the experts who are required to run the business for you E.g. you want to start a GMAT coaching centre, now either you have cracked the GMAT yourself and you know the whole process OR you have some identified employees who can do it for you who have been doing this time and again OR you have a co-founder who is an expert in this business. Your experts coaches will be the pillars of your business to start with, you should have that clarity from the day 1.

    b. If you do not have a technical expertise to run a particular business than you should have the business acumen to run the business and hire the right kind of human capital/co-founder. This drastically reduces the chances of your failure else in such kind of business , a shift in your human capital can possibly collapse your whole business.
23. **Market Entry Barriers :** e.g. you want to start a digital marketing agency, unless and until you know this business and you know how it operates plus you have some existing customers identified customers who are willing to pay for your services don't get into this business. The biggest reason is that there are no market barriers for anyone to start this kind of business, it doesn't require a herculean understanding or technical learning/expertise so you might hit into pricing crunch with respect to a lot of competition in the market from freelancers/agencies etc. So you should do your homework and market feasibility before getting into a generic business which does not have a lot of market entry barriers
24. **Build The Product/Services Roadmap**: Before you actually think about starting your business:
    a. You should write down the validation process and journey on what are the kind of milestones that you need to achieve or win.
    b. This would form the preface of your total business plan if you actually jump into the business.
    c. These milestones should have strict timelines to follow so that you work with deadlines and know that you have something tangible to achieve. Most of the entrepreneurs miss out on this and miss the bus as they so not have a pre defined roadmap to go to and achieve.
25. **Build Your Business Idea Board:** Prepare your business idea board very early in your business idea stage so that during the validation process you can start highlighting the key pointers and revisit them now and then. This will be a perfect revision and validation for you.

26. **Networking : Reach Out To Your Network :** Test the idea and their understanding of the business with your friends, peers, family, whoever you are comfortable in reaching out to. Don't Shy at all, The more people you reach out to , the more perspective will you get for the business idea. As i said before don't get carried away with critical remarks, those remarks and suggestions might be good for you to to rethink your product/services roadmap.
27. **Do You Have Complete Clarity In What You Are Trying To Achieve**: Only once you are clear in your milestones of validation process you should go ahead. You should have absolute clarity in terms of the following for your business :
    a. What you are planning to do ?
    b. How do you plan to execute it ?
    c. When do you plan to start it ?
    d. Where are you planning to start it ?
    e. Who are your target audience ? Do they want to buy your product/services ?
    f. Is this business financially feasible ?
    g. How is the competition doing it ?
28. **Operational Break Even :** While you are validating your startup business idea you should also keep this in mind that when are you breaking even on the operational expenses. This will help you in streamlining and validating how much funds you might require to run your business and when are you expecting to get into revenue positive stages E.g. The total Operating Expenses for your business might be the following:
    a. Working Capital
    b. Fixed Expenses like software, hardware etc
    c. Variable Expenses like salaries, incentives electricity etc
    d. Overhead Expenses

Now let us assume the Total Operating Expenses is X per month for your business.

Let us assume your projected revenue is Y per month.

You will operationally breakeven when Y becomes greater than X.

Complete Breakeven: You will attain a complete break even when your revenues will be able to cover the operating costs along with all expenses that have been put into the business including one time costs as well e.g. Infrastructure building costs etc.
- Let us assume the Total Operating Expenses is X per month for your business.
- Let us assume the Total One Time Costs like Infra and Development Costs is B. Let us say we amortize this cost over a period of 12 months so this becomes B/12 = Z per month
- Now your fully loaded costs per month is B + Z
- Let us assume your projected revenue is Y per month for your business
- You attain a complete break even when Y is greater than B + Z or Y - (B + Z) = Positive

29. **Stage Of Funds**: Last not the least this is super critical to evaluate the following for your business post your validation stage, you should have a defined idea if not the complete evaluation:
    a. How much funds would require to run the venture for at least 18 months?
    b. Do you have enough funds to sustain the first stage-12 months ?
    c. Have you built your cost vs revenue planning ?
    d. Have you planned your next rounds of funds ?
    e. When would you require funds, What stages ?
    f. Have you identified the investors who might be interested ?
    g. Have you built your pitch deck ?
    h. Is Your Go To Market for investors ready ?
    i. Are you investor ready yourself ?

" Stay Patient and Trust Your Journey"
---- Anonymous

" Outstanding People Have One Thing In Common : An Absolute Sense Of Mission"

---- Zig Ziglar

Notes That You Should Take
"Final Pointers For Startup Business Validation That You Should Know"

- Don't Overlook Critical Things During Validation Process
- Know The 5 Buckets Of Your Idea Validation
- Prefer Working In Your Areas Of Interest
- Insource Your Ability Area Work, Outsource Your Weak Areas
- **Answer Cleary** : Who, Why, When, Where, What & How ?
- There Are No Shortcuts To Success
- Try Business Model Canvas Approach
- Build A Product Life Cycle Board
- Forget Spreadsheets If You Want, Work Practical
- Have Customers Who Will Work With You
- Do Your Market Research To Get Realistic Data
- Build A MVP/Prototype, Go To Market, Early, Fast
- Hire A Mentor Or Advisor On Board
- Don't Rush Into Things
- Trust Diligently On Everyone
- Hire Teams Only When You Need Them
- Choose The Right Co-Founders
- Better To Have Competent Human Capital
- Build The Right Legal Documentation During Validation
- Talk To Existing Entrepreneurs, Take Feedbacks
- Do You Have The Ability To Pull Off The Business ?
- Know Your Market Entry Barriers
- Build Your Product/Services Roadmap
- Build Your Business Idea Board
- Reach Out To Your Networks
- Do You Have Clarity In What You Are Trying To Achieve ?
- Know Your Operational/Complete Breakeven
- You Should Know The Stage Of Funds For Sustenance

A Little Prayer (Note To Self)

Now that you are all set, revise whatever notes you have made and the questions you have written. Try to answer all the questions you had noted with respect to your startup business idea.

Start with your basic business validation process of your startup idea with people, data, experience, market etc. This is going to be a long long journey, here is a small prayer for your journey. This has always been my Note To Self for new journeys in life :

O God, O Lord,
To Thee I Pray,
Increase My Knowledge,
Day By Day.

If you like this book please feel free to share your reviews and feedback and also share this book with someone who could benefit from it. I would also love to connect with you on LinkedIn or Twitter.

Bon Voyage, My Friend :)

" You Don't Have To Be Great To Start But Have To Start To Be Great"

---- Zig Ziglar

www.ingramcontent.com/pod-product-compliance
Lightning Source LLC
Chambersburg PA
CBHW071055240526
45469CB00006BD/2303

I don't read fiction books, I will only eat vanilla ice cream, I hate oriental foods or anything spicy, been playing chess since I was 6, I read the encyclopedia when I was 8 in over a week, summer of '94 I read every psychology book the Jackson Co. Public Library had, in college for computer programming I made the presidential list in two months, I know how to build virtual machines, I can repair the hardware on any computer or printer, I know the pressures for R-22 and 410A, I can electrically wire anything, my favorite science is astrophysics, I think quantum physics is humanity's sick attempt to infuse religion with science, I believe I can construct a self-sustaining energy source... I am weird. For some reason I have an insane ability to analyze anything with precision, break it down in seconds and already know how to perfect it. I learn quickly, I don't bullshit and I have a control over my thoughts that amazes even me at times. For example once when I was smaller I was able to control my dreams. I was able to control anything and everything, an entire world that I could play with. The last time I was able to do it I took it a little too far and built an entire air force base with hundreds of jets, hangers, tunnels and defensive capabilities. I could have sworn I was dreaming for weeks, it was only 8 hours and I woke up right before takeoff in my first jet. For months I tried going back, I never could and for years i never could control my dreams the same again, until one night. When I was 15-16 I went to sleep as normal and when I "awoke" I actually was in the cockpit of that jet I never got to fly. I was flying for hours, in and out of clouds, seeing the water drops slide off the glass, feeling the G's on my chest as I did loops and feeling dizzy like my throat was in my stomach, it was the best experience of my life dreaming. I never went back, I never could control my dreams the same. Now it's just random whatever's that just keep me entertained but something did remain. It gave me an insight into how you used your brain. I thought, if dreams were some constructs of perceptions that felt like reality... then by thinking differently we controlled our reality. How I began all this and where I thought would be a good start was religion. Now with over 3000 different ones, obviously this would take some time.

13 years ago I came upon something I could not figure out, god. What a topic for me to pick, since I claimed intelligence, this would be a perfect test of my ability. So I tried... and failed, many, many, many times. I did come up with one scenario so wild it would have made scientology foam at the mouth. Though, it couldn't explain the soul's makeup or how it transitioned into another plane... so I scraped it. You see I don't use emotion to search for logic, I think that's stupid but what do I know? I never got a piece of paper from what the department of education deemed to be knowledgeable or relevant in the subjects in which I studied. Screw'em, I don't need their recognition to say I was a good boy who paid some money and took their tests. Knowledge is a choice and I chose to lean every single part of biology, geology, paleontology, chemistry, genetics, physics, astronomy and all the other cross sciences like biochemistry or astrophysics simply by going to the library guys. I never had a mother that held me, told me things were ok; I had a mother that called me stupid, a stepfather who used me as a punching bag and friends that laughed at the tough guy always talking about science. I learned how to take emotion and change it into whatever I needed it to be and I learned how achieving pure clarity finds absolute logic. For years I read every single "Standing on the Shoulders of Giants" and "Origin of Species" book I could find, along with the bibles from Buddha, Jewish, Muslim, Shinto, Mormon, Catholic/Christian and even Voodoo religions. Despite it all, I still was nowhere close to finding anything on life's creation. Until one day, one simple question that I never thought to ask, one single molecule that blew all of the other theories, away... just blew them all away... and I couldn't believe what I was looking at. See the reason no one has come up with it this way is because were a race of one doer's. We will devote our ENTIRE LIVES TO ONE PROFESSION, stupid. However, if there were more say, bio-geneticists, maybe someone would have figured it out and found it by now.

What I found and explain here will test the very comprehension methods you use today and stretch every fiber of faith you ever had. At first it will seem so preposterous, so insane that you'll think I've gone completely mad but I haven't. I have tried to discredit it, believe me but I figured out god. I know how life got here, I know how the soul is created, I know the purpose of all existence and I know god had nothing to do with any of it. Why would I want to isolate myself and drive everyone I cared about completely away labeling me an enemy to religion you ask?? I have no freaking idea, all I did was read some books and didn't use perception to construct reality. Getting mad at me for showing you the obvious isn't my fault, I just work here, if you want to believe in talking snakes and magic trees... that's cool, just don't complain about the world when death unexpectedly takes someone you love and you couldn't possibly understand the reasoning behind it. I am very direct, honest but above all truthful and I don't care who's feelings I hurt expressing those actions. Look around, obviously something isn't working right. Is this a magical being's sick joke of recognition worship or would it be an organization designed to keep the labor in line by promising equality only achieved after a lifetime of servitude? Maybe we should ask the Romans or a free thinking woman? Maybe we should grow up and stop believing in ancient fairy tales our ancestors reasoned events outside their understandings. I mean social structure has not even changed one bit since the Stone Age... wonderful... that makes us still cavemen. Trusting in religion over the years has gotten us nothing but war, death and misery... citing human unification, intelligence and scientific studies were evil. Well of course they are, they got a business to run and that would be bad for profits.

First thank you to my wife Tina and all of you reading, you took time to hear what I had to say and I thank you for that. To my wife, thank you for the support (despite her insane religious views) I'll always love you my wife. I'd like to dedicate this book to Mr. Charles Darwin (hence the title) and my kids and all of yours, to our future. This is to Darwin and all the others who believed giving their lives (not for personal self-gain) for the betterment of all humanity was the right thing to do— this is for you, take a bow, you've earned it gentlemen. We should have holidays honoring them, instead of some cracked out bunny laying eggs everywhere or the fat guy sliding all lubed up down a chimney in the dead of winter, right, when people would most likely be using their fireplaces, yeah that's smart. You wonder why the world is so messed up... hmm I do wonder that sometimes. I'm not trying to say I figured everything out but I figured everything out. I found how life used molecular dioxide osmosis to construct itself. I understand the constructs of a soul and its role in awareness. I know why humans evolved while others remained in the trees and I figured out that the stories of Moses, Noah and Adam were of one massive single event and not 3 separate ones. I'll show you how genetics is tied to chemistry, how chemistry's tied to biology, how it's all reliant on physics and how astronomy holds it all together. Calling me an atheist would be incorrect for I do believe in something, science and I'm not trying to destroy anyone's higher whatever I'm just trying to grow our race up a little.

It seems the irony of one's fate resides from the choices in which they make themselves.

Welcome to Darwin's Genesis

Chapters

Creation though Mutation

Organic Planetary Surgery

Molecular Dioxide Osmosis

Genetics Power Source

Cerebral Sensory Awareness

Adaptation to Evolution

Cognitive Cerebration Synthesis

Yin Verses Yang

Rise of Primates

Observation towards Eradication

Great Simian War

Erectus' Epic Odyssey

Fall of Eden

Purification thru Manipulation

The Sapient Virus

Religious Industrial Complex

Their Secret War

Destruction

then

Resurrection

The Scientific Revolution

Surviving the Epidemic

Achieving Humanitarian Maturity

Beyond Our Reality

Prepping for Surgery

A planets condition is very important to spawn life. Science tells us it's their belief that water is the catalyst, along with the distance from the sun that makes life appear. However water and distance is important, there are far more factors needed for life to spawn.

First, the elements needed in abundance are Hydrogen, Oxygen, Nitrogen and Carbon. These elements are then combined based on certain factors a planet must have. First factor is a rocky planet with a core which is needed for elements to remain close enough together in one region, allowing them to bond together into complex compounds. Also important is the landscape needed for water to form in pools of a liquid state for transmissions and osmosis of DNA. This is only possible if the planet has a core hot enough to produce magma, which is effected by the elements that make it up and the amount of pressure applied from gravities force towards the center of the planet's core.

Second is an atmosphere which is needed for pressurization, helps regulate temperatures and for moisture transportation. Another use is its ability to block or trap the suns lethal radiation which can drastically affect temperatures and wind speeds. Distance from the sun is somewhat important for heat absorption, however it depends heavily on the atmosphere how a planet gains and loses heat radiation as well. Also the size of the planet plays a role to, the more surface area exposed to light will greatly affect its absorption on heat.

Third is water. Needed primarily for the osmosis of H_2O and C_4N_2, it plays a huge role in the building of the genes. It protects them from the radiation of the sun before the ozone (O_3) was created. Another main function of water is its amazing conductive and resistive properties to electrons. While able to transmit them with ease, water's also an excellent grounding source by completely touching the ground allowing for a path of least resistance.

The fourth factor is lightning. This factor is the hardest for it relies heavily on the other factors to be present. When we have a heart attack, the proper method to start it again is a surge of electrons pumped into it. This is the catalyst; this one factor starts a chain reaction making a simple molecule into a singular conscientious able to store and release electrons. In order for life to get even further than a single molecule, aside from the 4 main factors and elements listed here, certain complex compounds and processes are also needed in the evolving of DNA. Granite is an important requirement, without it the process would never start. Once it starts it needs methane and ammonia to sustain, construct and inject onto the genome by processing amino acids from conditions on earth.

Essentially the most important part to building DNA is amino acids and would be the fifth factor. These compounds is what makes DNA possible for they contain the elements that build most of the genes and is what's needed for replication and functionality of the helix. Amino acids do a lot in DNA and are produced naturally and did so on earth w/o our genes breaking methane and ammonia down first. In an experiment done in 1950's called the Miller-Urey experiment where they created a controlled environment that was similar to earth's at that time life spawned, filled it with methane and ammonia... and waited. Sure enough, amino acids produced however there experiment, at the time, didn't hold water. They theorized the molecules were formed in the atmosphere and the energy needed to breakdown and build amino acids wasn't feasible, while lightning was common it didn't strike enough to build the scale needed for life production.

They were close, so close... they didn't put it all together yet... the energy didn't come directly from lightning, it came from C_4N_2. It is funny to note that these guys even had to prove this theory. Where did they think amino acids came from... magic?? The science community should be ashamed of their reasoning behind discovering the origins to life or lack thereof. Their objective ways has caused their reasoning to be deliberately altered; mostly I believe it's their faith, perceptional driven is their process of learning this truth... simply they let faith dictate what they learn. Instead of taking their experiment and running with it they try desperately to prove it wrong or refuse to accept what it suggest. They took a giant leap forward learning how DNA acquires its elements to produce itself and they want to argue over the exact conditions on earth. You never thought it was the genes that evolved first? From a single molecule into a genetic structure... did you smart guys every think of that?? Impossible, it has to be magical, right? From a telescope to a microscope, no where do you see magic, all you see is cause and effect.

I'll show you in the next chapter the last factor and how life does it but you see today how diversified life is and how rapidly it grows and spreads once conditions are met. It is not hard to understand that we, in the void of space, are defiantly not alone. As it turns out we're actually late to the party and most of the events are long and over with. You got to remember the earth is only 4.5 billion years old… that's only when it had formed on the outskirts of our galaxy… the universe had galaxies a lot larger than ours turning and spinning billions of years before the Milky Way began forming stars near its core. This actually would be pretty cool to see; even how the mood was formed, an asteroid the size of about Mercury side-swiping earth knocking a chunk off which eventually cooled.

From geology records of ice core samples taken in the artic, they show earth having very violent climate and its ability and inability to support life changed constantly. Just looking at the landscape, we can see large crater impacts indicating massive damage at once. Also just look at the moon with its anything but smooth surface. This should tell us how fragile our climate is and its effects on life on earth. It appears, from the ice cores, our climate will eventually rip itself apart and devastate our way of life just like it has done at least 5 times already. Mostly the atmosphere is the cause where it can trap heat either from a meteor or volcanic activities polluting it. Based on the atmosphere's elemental makeup determines how much light reaches the surface which regulates a planets temperature. Regardless, the atmosphere is vital in producing the genes but that all depends on the planets gravity, surface area exposed to light and rotational velocity. Where gravity pushes gases down, compresses it, traps it from escaping and makes an atmosphere. This causes atmospheric pressure and depending on the element, determines the density which in turn, will affect wind speed. The surface area directly effects density by how much its spread out the gas and how much light is absorbed.

An atmosphere's ability to reflect or absorb light from its star is a very fragile and very important factor for the creation of life to form for it brings liquid water and regulates temperature. By combining dust particles and water vapor to make clouds which helps to absorb light, create heat and can form amino acids. Also equally important, it allowed the water vapor to combine together, rise up from the heat, reach the edge of space where heat dissipates rapidly. Then cools and condenses from the loss of heat causing rain to fall to the surface and pools of liquid water began showing up. If the surface wasn't solid, like a gas planet, liquid water could not form in pools like earth making a planets core pretty important for life as well. Because of clouds, the catalyst is able to generate lightning and would strike the surface. Sometimes it would hit water, sometimes it wouldn't but with earth ability to strike several times a day it's only a matter of time until it hits an area that has the molecules needed for life to spawn.

As you can see, there is far more factors needed for life to evolve besides water and distance from the sun. Climate plays the biggest role, however the elements that make up the planet are also a big part of that. As you progress through my book I will show you how all these factors come into play in the creation of life naturally and without the use of a magical being. By thinking logically and using reasoning to look at the conditions that led to this reality we perceive to be real, will help you understand our purpose, our fate and who we are. Life is precious and very rare but we must preserve our survival, not our culture. What good will cultures do if we're extinct? The most important part I believe is vital to our survival is realizing god has no control in reality...none. The events that occur in the universe are a result of causes and effects. What this will do for us is make us realize our future is in our own hands. That we will start taking responsibility for our actions and our children's future, in order to survive... this is the whole damn point to life. Sitting around and saying whatever happens is god's will is like having a lion run towards you hungry rationalizing god put the animal there to eat you. Believing global warming is a myth from people's goal of financial gain, is insane. Do we have to show you how greenhouse gasses work? Do we have to tell you we can't breathe CO_2? How important the ice caps and the ozone are? Is this a big joke to you? You think capitalism will save you when plants won't grow outside anymore... and what will we tell our children when they can't breathe the air anymore or drink the water? We liked paper currency so much we said screw the environment?? The people who believe pumping CO_2 gases in the air while wiping out all of earths forest has nothing to do with greenhouse gases causing warmth, are the same people who say science is too hard for them to understand... no wonder you believe them, you don't have a damn clue. What happened to our race when we stopped learning for ourselves and let others provide the information we want? Easy to say god is in control, that way we're not responsible for our actions... keeps us from feeling guilty when we hand the world over to our children, right? Makes me sick to my stomach; gods will... I'll show you how god is the real myth with Molecular Dioxide Osmosis.

Molecular Dioxide Osmosis

The thing religion could explain that no one else could was the creation of life. Science didn't know the process, history couldn't pinpoint where and why and for years I struggled with this. Coming up with theory after theory I would debunked each one as quickly as I got it until one day I was left with was nothing and gave up. Now for me, I love science but chemistry wasn't really my strongest skillset but genetics used chemistry a lot and I thought by learning chemistry it would help me understand how genetics worked. Boy was I right... one day I was looking at the makeup to the genes and their elemental structure. I kept trying to find clues on its origin and couldn't ever quite grasp it, until I finally asked the right question. See it's not the answers that we search for in science; it's the right question we constantly are struggling to find. I asked myself if man evolved ape to man, why wouldn't DNA? It smacked me like a huge sledgehammer because the answer had been staring at me the entire time I just hadn't asked question. I kept thinking the genes arrived here then built the helix but they didn't arrive, they were built here also.

Looking at the genome and the genes I noticed a pattern. In the middle of every gene, in every helix there was a molecule that was exactly the same. It consisted of 4 carbon and 2 nitrogen atoms (C_4N_2). This was chemistry's realm right here. Skeptically, I said "Ok, so if this molecule is the key then it has to be produced naturally and in abundance here on earth." so I looked it up...C_4N_2 is a linear (Meaning straight) molecule formed when hot granite touches nitrogen gas and produces it. As you should know, all continents' we live on are granite underneath and the atmosphere consist of 96% nitrogen gas... I couldn't believe what I was reading. I didn't think it was that easy, that simple and if it was why haven't... why was I the only one who found this molecular dioxide osmosis? Religion, I am not affected by it. I know god doesn't exist and I didn't need science to prove that to me, I just didn't think it was that simple. Now for any who are not familiar with physics or chemistry, look this next part up later cause you probably won't understand any of it. My best example of an atom and how it works is to take a solar system and shrink it; they move, act and look almost exactly the same and are governed by the same laws of matter and energy. As our planet formed and cooled it formed a crust along the circumference. It started releasing gases and making our atmosphere, spreading all around. Gas elements like H_2O,

O2, CO2, N2, CH4 and NH3 (Water, oxygen, carbon dioxide, nitrogen, methane and ammonia) began mixing thru a sort of static electrification soup in the atmosphere where the sun breaks the bonds of molecules. This releases the electrons by their attractions to light, builds them up in groups that produce some unstable results. Random small discharges in the atmosphere would spark up, high in voltage but low amps from the density of the atmosphere providing resistance plus it was a grounding source. This charged the atmosphere making the compounds of amino acids thru low electrification.

When surges of electrons are applied to already unstable molecules charged by light, their shared electrons will scatter more easily, breaking the bond that holds them to other element. This temporary loss of electrons allows molecules to bond in different ways making new more complex compounds. These are the amino acids that the Miller/Urey experiment proved in the 50's. These compounds then attached themselves to water droplets and gravity pushed them down to the surface… making earths first oceans enriched in amino acids. As it did the atmosphere became less dense, causing it to lose its grounding source it was using which caused a massive buildup of static electricity. These "bolts" of discharge rained down in huge numbers, striking almost every inch of surface area on the planet. This included the newly formed oceans which was doing its own thing as well. As C4N2 formed in the oceans, at first simple and non-living, it would be electrified by the bolts striking the water. As water is a great conductor, being completely on the ground made it an even better resistor as well. This shielded C4N2 from the intensity and applied a low electrical charge to the molecule. This caused it to curl as to attempt to ground itself out by the electron outer shell reacting to the negative polarity surge applied by the lightning and repelling away. This made C4N2 make a circle and at the same time did something unexpected as well, become a battery.

This is where life, the spirit If you will, comes from. See as it connected, the electrons were on their way out and to them they just kept going in a circle, preventing the energy from leaving. This would store the energy and not allow it to escape, going in a sort of marry-go-round. This would make it alive, well not really alive as it was electrified, but it was making it able to move. By moving it would run into water molecules and would transfer some of the electrons at water and break their bonds. Through osmosis, C4N2 would acquire the hydrogen and oxygen elements by applying low electrical charges to H2O and infusing them together through molecular dioxide osmosis and doing the exact same thing the atmosphere did to make amino acids. By acquiring more molecules and constructing the genes it made DNA. The bigger it got, the more energy it was able to store and produce more effects by altering the way the electron wave is released. Due to the genes molecular manipulation, electrons forced across it would cause the wave to alter from the molecules different elements and their different repulsion rates.

Something to note is it "understands" by gaining more molecules to break down other molecules, it grows bigger and able to store and apply more energy. This allows for more complex and precise actions and movements but as it applies the energy it loses it too, slowing it down. Therefore gaining more energy was required to survive therefore, its primary goal is acquiring more molecules. To survive it must break them down and gain their energy to sustain for if it stops completely, it will die. This is where life gets its main primary instinct, survival. All DNA on this and any other planet does just two things for survival, store electrons... then... release the electrons in a controlled directed way to produce an action based on the elemental makeup of the gene used. This concept of death or self-awareness is something all life shares from bacteria to humans and is what we claim as a soul... I'll explain that later but for now let's just say our perception of a soul is way off. Now let me say this about life; it is far from perfect. C4N2's ability to build onto itself didn't always go exactly as planned. Matter of fact nature is anything but perfect, I'm not sure where we got the idea that it is.

Mutations are a roll the dice and see what sticks, there is no plan... it has more to do with environment and the elements contained in it than some ultimate design. Mutation is just another proof that in nature (reality) things aren't designed, they're not planned and nature as well as life is the results of cause and effect from the smallest to the largest level. They all follow the same rules, the same methods, same patterns because they are made of the same thing... atoms. Because warm, freshly formed granite ran into an area releasing nitrogen gas pumping into the atmosphere it created life on our planet. By the effects of attraction and repulsion it made a linear molecule that when electrified, is able to make a simple molecule into a "biological battery" able to store and release energy... becoming "alive".

Something interesting about the chemical makeup of DNA is the life molecules arrangement. When it's energized, because nitrogen is on the ends, it curls but the surge is what causes the nitrogen to flip with the carbon making NCNCCC from NCCCCN. The reason for this is amazing from nitrogen's N2 bond that is the strongest bond in the known universe. However by itself, it is very energy hungry while carbon on the other hand is not. These two elements are the bonding ones to the other gene. What that means is electrons travel down the helix's middle if hits nitrogen it's sucked in, if its carbon it bounces off making the on/off switch coding we see today. This is the connection no one made, how C4N2 was able to store and release electrons in a way to produce a reaction to other molecules in order to gain more electrons and allowing it to survive. This is what we call the circle of life; biology repeating the same actions over and over again in a loop process by absorbing and releasing energy to adapt. In the next chapter I will show how electron wave motion plays into all of this but the whole process of life creation is all possible from how light will attract electrons on a planet. By degrading the molecules thereby collecting, compressing causes concentrating them in a bolt of discharge but that isn't the best part. Actually C4N2 (in my opinion) isn't as interesting as how feelings work and how our concept of a soul has been completely misinterpreted. But in order to get to that point we have to explore energy in the world of physics first to understand the source behind biology's use of energy, behind Genetics Power Source.

Generic's Power Source

Charles Darwin was an explorer and actually not the best in his field. Mostly because he went to some weird places but, I believe if only he had been a geneticist he would have been famous. Darwin didn't care about religion or carbon dating fossils; he didn't care about others perception on what they validate as reality or was trying to discredit what anyone felt. He cared about one thing, showing the world that nature will improve itself through trial and error of adaption, (different arrangement of genes on the genome) otherwise called evolution, to survive. What I've found through biology, geology, chemistry, physics, psychology, paleontology, astronomy and genetics is that nut job, Darwin, that everyone thought was a waste of time... not only... was he right, we had no idea how right he really was and how wrong (ONCE AGAIN) we all really are. How magic is really caused by a natural process based on variables and the elements involved. Resulting in predictable effects that are repeated and re-worked in a way to better itself... always... in all life.

From the laws of motion mentioned by Newton we see how attraction and repulsion will strip or bond the outer electron shells of elements sometimes releasing electrons. However, unlike light's motion, electrons travel circular and almost stay suspended (revolving around in the same spot) until attracted or repelled by an opposite or equal polarity. In biology there's no difference in their motion, the difference is DNA doesn't use sunlight to acquire its electrons. Let me clarify before I continue... life doesn't know what it's doing, it has no reasoning at this level to know. What it's doing is reacting to an action applied to it by the attractions and repulsions of the atoms sub-atomic particles that make it up. Matter (atoms) consists of 2 charged particles, the Proton (+) and the Electron (-) and a neutral particle, the Neutron, without a charge and not attracted by any polarity. W/o going into physics too much, there is no difference between matter and energy except energy is in motion. The most common form of matter transfer is electrons, where electrons are compressed together and flow to the nearest conductor to neutralize across an elements electron shell.

All stable atoms have electrons moving around them fast. As the elements nucleus (middle) gets bigger with more protons and neutrons, this allows for more electrons to circle around it. Each time it gets bigger a new shell can hold more electrons. Now to visualize it's just like a solar system; Shell 1 (Mercury) = 2 electrons maximum, Shell 2 (Venus) = 8 maximum, Earth=32 and so on. Depending on the elements core, determines its ability to attract or repel electrons making them conductive or insulating.

That is the advantage C4N2 has over all other molecules, its ability to store extra electrons within itself and still able to remain stable enough to transfer it to another molecule. Let me explain, like mentioned above, atoms are able to hold or transfer or resist electrons based on how many they have already. Nature LOVES balance but will deal with imbalances as long as it's not excessive. The Carbon in C4N2 is a good conductor and can bond together while storing extra electrons think of carbon as the glue and storage. Nitrogen is a little touchier as it is by itself and was split up from its natural form of N2 as it formed. As N2 it is the most stable combo in the entire universe, it is very hard to break. However by itself, it is electron hungry and wants to bond to anything. In C4N2 there is a carbon atom between the two nitrogen atoms making the nitrogen a very good transmitter for the molecule meaning, in its formation(NCNCCC), this molecule is able to absorb, store and then release electrons at matter but does it while still remaining intact and functional. The carbon/nitrogen combination is a perfect combo for resisting the effects of electrons surged onto it while still being able to store them as well.

By stimulating C4N2's ability to move it allowed it to bump into other molecules thereby transferring it's electrons towards it (Like a car stopping suddenly) into the molecule breaking it down and releasing the atoms which C4N2 absorbs storing more energy. By building onto it with the molecules, causes it to store more energy than before and allowing it to do more actions and travel further. Accidently it does this, meaning it doesn't know what it's doing. What it knows is it needs to always look for more energy to maintain itself or survive. When C4N2 would apply the electron charge, this is a simple action where releasing energy to other matter provides, depending on the matter, a certain reaction.

Now when you add resistance to the pathways, making the route more complex the electrons travel across, will manipulate the properties of the energy wave that's applied. Now the genes (there's 4 of them) connect together but only with the right one. The way this lock and key process works is two of the genes only connect with two elements, while the other pair connect to 3. On DNA, the genes are able to direct which gene to flow the energy across by resistance making the path of least resistance across the gene that wants it. This on/off type process of coding is similar to computer binary language of 0's and 1's. Interesting to note, the inventor of this language was an atheist who probably as well viewed our bodies as machines. Funny thing, by using electrical hardware components used in computers does help explain DNA's process for coding and using energy. As electrons flow across atoms they are manipulated by the elements properties like mass, ionic polarity and molecular arrangement. Transistors and resistors also manipulate energy based on what materials are used, how it releases the output and changes the effects when applied is the same way the gene's molecules arrangement also affects the electron wave flowing across. When more genes are combined and their outflow is applied together, evolved DNA to do more advanced actions and movements.

However the process of electrical coding by DNA will eventually decay the elements inside the gene and break down the helix. Just like a computer manipulating electrical currents to produce certain actions, DNA will also break down. By forcing electrons across molecules, they play hop scotch from atom to atom down the molecule. This causes resistance from the two same polarities (Electrons) and will eventually break the bonds of the molecule or decay the elements themselves, stripping their electrons and making them unstable. The need to replenish or regenerate was vital for DNA to survive. This is when life developed A-sexual reproduction. See life like's patterns and routines, set ways and schedules; on how things are done. This is so life can focus on evolving better abilities like sense's to navigate better. If there are irregularities in its primary function of energy consumption, it must secure that first above all other priorities. The problem with A-sexual is it makes a copy, of a copy, of a copy and by the 100th or so generation there is data corruption or lose and was catastrophic in forming higher level organisms but for simple low level organisms it didn't matter as much. When groups of genomes are combined and used to perform complex data transfers (higher level) like an ability to receive signals instead of always discharging them required reproduction to be perfect in order to remain stable and life evolved bi-sexual reproduction. By combining 2 RNA strands together this ensured better copying by less to copy from scratch and just filling the missing pieces from the remaining RNA strands, giving diversity to life. This, "receiving skill", was the fundamentals for life's ability to interpret and react, based on signals coming towards it. With a stored, programmed response it made life's sensory perception. Part 4 will go deeper into life's reason for advancing the genetic structure as to increase its abilities to adapt and survive. Again, evolution plays into biology making it able to store electrons. Then, direct them across a set pattern of pre-arranged elements by osmosis, influencing the energies motion from this arrangement, able to apply different motion's based on the arrangement of the elements it travels across.

In short.. life is the ability for a molecule (C4N2) to store and release a surge of electrons based on the elements it's made of which can be used to make an action which causes an equal or opposite reaction. By grouping and infusing more elements to it with amino acids and water in sets and arranged differently made the genes and allowed for more complex actions. By applying energy and losing the energy by actions it "realizes" its need to acquire more energy by slowing down as it runs out. This is life's fundamentals for survival or replenishment of electrons through the breakdown of molecules by applying stored energy to them. Starting with the original molecule, C4N2, with the help of water and amino acids created a molecule able to apply stored energy to produce an action by releasing it... this created life and does so throughout the universe. Time has no meaning and isn't some fabric able to manipulate or re-construct. Not too sure where Einstein was going with the fabric of space/time. Einstein was wrong, the fabric Einstein was trying to figure out was actually gravity. Without going into astrophysics too much, just like protons and electrons, energy comes in two forms of polarities... positive and negative. Einstein didn't go simple enough, thus resulting in asking the wrong questions... if light is energy which can't be created or destroyed, what's the opposite of it?

If light has a polarity, let's say positive, what is the negative? To comprehend this we must first classify light by characterizing it. For 1, light always emits away from its source... for 2, when it comes in contact with an atom its electrons are attracted and expands away from its nucleus. In molecules this changes their states of matter from a solid to a liquid, liquid to a gas and eventually to plasma. Now to find the opposite to that we need a force that emits towards its source and makes matter contract or compress its electrons by repelling them. By comparing a solar system to an atom I was able to find lights opposite force... gravity. Gravity emits from the poles of a planet, circle's the perimeter, meets in the middle and goes towards its source. Now when it comes into contact with matter it "compresses" the electrons (probably from being the same polarity and repelling each other) and pushes them towards the nucleus of atoms. Which on a planet as they fall from the sky towards the core, being repulsive, it pushes all matter towards the core as well. I'm not too sure where science got gravitational pull from and it being the weakest force the universe. I don't see light moving or holding together our solar system or perhaps turning a galaxy. Since we finally figured out black holes were in the center of stars and galaxies… maybe… that's how solar systems are formed and why nebulas start rotating and compressing all of its elements together to a centralized spot in the middle of a circling nebula. Causing the atoms to be forced together in fusion and splits the nucleus which causes fission, creating a star.

By actually studying light and the reactions it has with matter, you notice light, not as a creator of anything but actually much like a wrecking ball that degrades matter and breaks its molecular bonds. While gravity is much like a trash compactor, puts it all back together… without going into physics too much. Throughout all of my research of the universe and life I have always seen ONE absolute constant across all scientific fields of matter and energy, nature and a conscience; they all operate in cycles from its primary rule of balance. When something is unbalanced, it will destroy itself only to remake itself in a different, more balanced way. That is the point of life for it owes its survival from the rules of balance. It is because of this rule life is able to hold, sustain and create a self-awareness ability used to interact with its environment, we call the soul.

Based on the rules of balance, life begins to break down from using the energy. The molecules in the genes eventually will disperse, causing the need for better survival instincts that all life shares. Now it is my belief that viruses were in fact not the first technically life-form, they are life's first attempts in reproduction. My example is the immune system and how it kills viruses, so how does it? Well when I was little and wanted to be a microbiologist and kill viruses. I found it fascinating how our medicines didn't kill them our immune system did so I had to study it extensively. What I learned confused me a bit since I thought viruses weren't alive. So first let's classify life by what it does; all life will eat, grow, adapt, create waste, reproduce and eventually die. This includes humans, dogs, fish, worms, bacteria and yes virus's too. Now it is believed that viruses are attacking their hosts, I think that's wrong, to me it looks like their confused and seeking balance. Our white blood cells offer that balance by matching the genetic sequence of the opposite side. See there's DNA and RNA, the difference is

RNA is half of DNA and viruses only have RNA. All other life in the form of molecules consist of DNA, except them. What is interesting is when the white blood cell attaches itself to a virus it will match its code opposite of it and makes it dormant.

      This gave me a perception of life as a machine where bits of code were manipulated by molecular sequencing, along a rotating helix set to produce a certain outcome. Based on the energy signatures registered the mind will interpret and interact to the signal creating life's first Cerebral Sensory Awareness

Cerebral Sensory Awareness

        This one was difficult to even comprehend, let alone explain self-awareness or the essence of a soul. My first clue was, if you can believe this, Mr. Joseph Stalin of the USSR. During the cold war Stalin wanted in on genetics so he could create the ultimate soldier by mixing their DNA and cross breeding apes with women… it was a complete failure. One experiment did grab my attention where he was going to put a human head on an ape's body, bypassing the cross-breeding failures. The first trial run was with 2 apes, one brain dead in a coma but fully alive. The other was in perfect condition and totally conscious. He switched their heads and attached the nerves. Very primitively, they were able to connect some and not all nerves and the coma ape with the others head… woke up. Not only awake but conscious and was able to feed himself, with its hand a few grapes before dying. It was a success but in a way never intended at all and not too many people actually get what he in fact did. By switching their heads, he switched their conscious and transferred a soul from one body to another. This was monumental in understanding what exactly a soul was and where it was however, it greatly depended on your definition of a soul and which creatures on earth had one.

        So… how does one classify a soul? Feelings and emotions, character and personality… Perhaps… it's Intelligence and reason that define the essence of a conscious? Probably the most puzzling is where did it come from if not a supernatural being? In human conception, at what point does a zygote acquire a soul? 99% of you do not know how to answer these questions except by using a higher being able to create them… for to understand a soul… is impossible… right? Before I quote the Matrix, you must remember this one truth… there is no spoon. What is "real"? How do you define "real"? If you define reality by what you see, smell, taste and touch then "real" is nothing more than electrical signals interpreted by your brain… electrical signals interpreted by your brain… prove it…Ok. As DNA grew near its limits of arrangements in genetic sequencing it started grouping strands together, making chromosomes, which gave them an advanced ability to send/receive more complex and detailed "electrical interpretations" and when applied to a certain groups of molecules, resulted in life's first creation of the cellular structure and the senses. This was everything for DNA because now it had a transport system as well as protection. It came with a price thou, far greater energy requirements which meant more energy consumption so

DNA needed a way to direct and map its movements by sensing where it's going and tracking where it has been.

By sending then receiving a signal and comparing what's different, chromosomes were able to interpret and mold to different signals from other molecules based on their specific electrical signature from their reaction to a cellular membrane shell. This evolutionary leap was able to protect DNA as well as send and transmit signals from the chromosomes to another molecule outside it. However, the main survival reason for this was life's ability to react to a signal with another transmit tainted signal back based on a reaction to its environment giving interpretation... like finding food or avoiding dangers... and thus the sense, touch was created from DNA's new ability in receiving electrical signals and comparing them to previous recorded signal's. Allowing it to "feel" what is around and helping ensure its survival, gave rise to the single and multicellular organisms whose primary goal was finding food and reproducing by sensing and reacting to its environment. As life advanced and was able to make different materials, they were used to sense touch in different ways by more complex signals like smells or sounds or even more advanced, sight.

All of the known senses to life derive from its touch ability interpreting different electrical signals from different materials used for transmitting the signals. The ability to sense the world, however remarkable, does not indicate or show what humans would call a soul, even a worm can sense pain, still says nothing in understanding our own self-awareness. Our soul has to be much more complicated or unique than a simple worm's ability to feel pain... right, maybe? Personality and reasoning is a good reference point to a soul, but a self-awareness ability to feel emotions would be a better reference to help us understand this. A personality is constructed from memories, which creates a perception that is used to interact with its environment. This influence's its reasoning which is life's ability to compare and analyze multiple signals, allowing for choices for survival all based from intelligence. This is what builds life's self-awareness to a soul.

I find it funny a lot when people ask if there is the 6th sense well maybe and if so, how about 7, 8 or 9?? We think there are 5 different senses life has when in fact there is actually only one sense all life has, touch. All the other senses uses touch but with different instruments, like an ear drum or an eye. Sound waves at different frequency touch the ear drum differently, so does the eye when different colors or shades of light touch it. To process it all, life needed a way to record the data to interpret them faster and allow for more accurate responses to the signals. As cells developed tissues and muscles it lead to organs and extremities for advanced movements and breaking down more complex molecules easier. Advancing the species sensory perceptions for them was vital to accurately operate and use their bodies to the best of its ability to ensure its survival. Spawning species with these new senses emerged from the animal cells that were developing them to better hunt for plants to eat. One of the organs developed was a ball of muscle able to copy and store different electrical signals much like DNA's chromosomes only the brain was able to classify the signals based from the intensity, the reaction to chemicals and which senses were used in transmitting them. It then indents the muscle exact to the signal and when it runs a blank signal across it, this will indent it and is how memory holds and recalls data, much like a hard drive in a computer where a platter is indented by similar factors.

The brain allowed life a faster ability to retain and recall information later in exact detail, giving life memories and developing reasoning. Different from instinct, memory is sensory imprinted while instinct is genetically mutated responses to the reactions from its environment. With the ability to retain and recall data or memories from any sensory transmitter, gave life reasoning, with species using a brain for storing these signals from its environment paved way for intelligence. With reasoning and intelligence together, life was able to interpret multiple signals at once as it happened and is the fundamentals for a species to construct a self-awareness state able to interact within its environment ... and made life's consciousness which has nothing to do with personality. Self-awareness is life's ability to construct a perceptional based reality from its interpretation of all senses used at that moment in order to advance its survival tactics. These reality memories are then compared to previous memories stored, giving life a sense of time and placement, which helps validate its existence from a feeling of contentment. This cypher's the multiple signals and allows life to choose which signals construct's its perception and making reality seam more real.

The two primary emotional states used to interpret a response, fear and contentment was life's way to apply a higher level of intensity to memories. This built its perceptions and making life self-aware and able to react to an action from its environment, based from its feelings of reality compared to its memories. Allowing life the ability to make choices that will direct its fate more by how it feels at a certain time... yeah, about time... I'm sorry all you quantum physics guru's, "time" is not a fabric or tangible object, Einstein was wrong. Time is a classification method all life uses to classify memories and/or a method used to predict future events, like changing seasons or when the sunrise will be, which helped in life's reasoning to its reality... So traveling through time I'm sorry no matter how badly you want it, you can't bring people back from the dead or save anyone.

Now the energy that biology uses, causing reactions and recording memories, is the exact same energy used to in our homes, shocks us back to life from heart failure and causes emotional responses. Life began storing more complex memories from multiple senses to better classify them on priority and needed a planned response to basic familiar signals in everyday life. By looping these responses while awake creates an identity from a built perception on its effects to others. Depending on similar memories and how they reflect towards others construct perceptions of good/evil, right/wrong. This gave life emotions to interpret the senses based on priority, intensity and creating "personality". Groups of related behaviors used to interact with others or actions that gives a sense of clarity. This gave life an ability to feel its environment much better. Aside from storing and accessing, this system resulted in faster, better and more complex responses to the multiple sensory signals the brain was using for reality. By recorded memories that were classified more, not just by perception of senses, but by priority from feelings of fear and happiness gave life different methods and abilities in its recording. Storing and recalling memories greatly improving life's motivations for survival and reasoning. However these motivational feelings depend heavily on how many memories a life form can classify, store and use when interpreting its reality. This greatly affects its emotional state of reasoning. Aside from logical, emotional reasoning gave life its primitive instincts for avoiding dangers and finding food by further classifying memories from prioritizing the signals, based from a perceptional construct of reality which interprets feelings of fear (bad=pain) or contentment (good=happiness). This helped life ensure its survival from its classification advancements in sensory perception, awareness and memory processing, recalling by improving the speeds of interactions with its environment. The results of this was relying on memory to produce a construct of multiple perceptions and leading to Cognitive Cerebration Synthesis of the soul and leading to what we call individuality.

Cognitive Cerebration Synthesis

This section will go deeper into the emotional side of life's reasoning and the importance of its development. As life developed more complex sense's its need to interpret them in different ways and was the primary factor leading to more in-depth reasoning of the environment in which we reacted with. This is what we humans call emotion and is an advanced method of sensing based on intensity. You see intensity was needed to become more accurate in our movements and reactions to the environment. The "feel" of an emotion is the level of importance of said sense that is registering the signal. For example, if you're swimming and the current is stronger than you, you get the feeling that your drifting and increased movement is needed to progress your current heading. For humans, emotion takes on a whole different meaning for we define it as our individuality which is what we classify us as unique and different from all other life on earth... even thou we are made of the same materials.

It's not that emotions are wrong or not supposed to happen but for humans we have taken it to an entirely wrong and misunderstood level. Religion has capitalized on this by using a technic used in motivational speaking where words are used with intensity to stimulate awareness and give a sense of energy in the air... so to speak. Emotions within life is an advanced method of cognitive (meaning memory perception) cerebration (meaning using the mind for processing) synthesis (combining these two processes from intensity levels) that develops a concise state of mind. First think of the concise and sub-concise states of awareness not two, but one. Think of it as the operating system for your senses and as far as the brain goes, the only examples I could find leading to any close conclusions was the computer. The way the brain accesses, compares and stores data is remarkably similar to a computer's hard drive, RAM and processor. The brain would follow the same concept as the computer but act like a muscle. Like any computer, prolonged exposers to energy will breakdown the bonds holding the components or molecules together. Insomnia can produce random images or noises that are not there, how is this possible and how sleep fixes it is rather interesting.

A biological entity will construct two different methods used for regulations of the body properly. It will transmit signals from pre-arranged chromosomes or will receive and interpret new signals. This entity does the same thing the genes did to evolve and regulate the flow of energy. The body breaks down complex compounds, molecular bonds; absorbs their electrons in the blood which is carried to the brain. The brain is a sponge soaking the energy up for storage, for the brain holds volatile data and cannot lose power for very long, about 7 minutes. However it is also imperative that it does not have a surge for the brains reasoning and classification system will malfunction and immediate shutdown is required or synapses will fry. Species with brains to function vitals and instinct do retain memory but more complex creatures construct perceptions of those memories. With that, therefor, insects do not feel fear or happiness but would experience pain or bad.

When a creature stores memories, classifying them is vital for reasoning and in order to process them better, the brain needs time to categorize them properly. If memory is rushed, sense's signals can get misinterpreted and things don't appear the way it should. Depending on how these signals are processed in the brain determines its conscious or sub-conscious states of awareness. Both are the same energies, just applied differently in a biological entity allowing to regulate the body by repeating the same signals in cycles or regeneration by comparing what's missing and fixing it. Regeneration however requires complete control of the signals as to provide treatment to any damaged or irregular cells. Interesting enough I believe I know how this happens. In computer backups there is a process called a snapshot where it take a picture and compares to previous pictures to match what's different, the body is the same. Where your snapshot is the coding in the cells chromosomes where a unique encoded signal is sent and if it gets a certain response it will continue on, if it's irregular than energy is diverted to it and replaces the anomaly, that is regeneration. These signals comes from different parts of the brain then the signals for the senses do and when asleep completely stops all sensory awareness communications. Think of your conscious as an operating system for a PC, like Windows. Improper shutdown can result in data corruption and a restart will throw errors. Like ROM, files like driving or eating can break down as they are accessed and a shutdown-restart is needed to reload the files, or sleeping as we call it. Dreams would be scripts running as the OS loads to run certain emotions, allow me to explain.

The conscious and sub-conscious state's is the way biology uses energy to repair and interact with the environment in order to survive. It's not that they are different in any way or separate from each other, they are just the direction of election flow within the body. Sleep is needed to power down the brain to repair the body and refresh the memory receivers and transmitters. As our bodies repair, the senses are shut off to allow for better signal flow to the cells. Just like a computer's RAM, where every time you shutdown then restart it is blank, a person's mood is as well when they start up. Like RAM, during the last moments of sleep, you enter what is called REM (Rapid Eye Movement) where your senses are not really on but your memory begins pulling random images and constructing a world inside your head. There is a purpose for dreams, to set you in a mood from your environment.

Wives will have dreams of a cheating spouse, teenage boys will have wet dreams, a girl will dream of a puppy she always wanted. These are some examples of how the mind uses dreams to set mood. People report, even me, waking up somewhere other than where they thought they should be. Back to the computer, RAM is volatile memory meaning if it loses power it loses the data. The hard drive is Non-volatile meaning it retains its data after power loss. A persons memories and their awareness, is the same volatile and non-volatile data in a hard drive (memory) and RAM (Awareness). As you wake up, your senses are powered on and you gain control of them but in a neutral state, clear and straight thru. This is because as you sleep all remaining important data from RAM is transferred to your HD or brain. Any leftovers are erased as the conscious loses power. As you come online your eyes begin rapidly moving back and forth as your being hacked. You see the way dreams feel so real is because the line feeding your cerebral awareness is overtaken by your memories, allow me to explain.

If you ever had a thought that consumed your mind, you would manifest it in your dreams and set an alarm as to keep you aware of the certain thought. The night before you sleep you set a sort of alarm for before you wake up. This constructs a world of pure essence and unimaginable power... a real Inception movie to you at least, only it's not real. This is your mind hacking itself by building a world from memory that produces a reaction based on the alarms instructions. For example, if you're sleeping in a hostile environment and you awake neutral, your chances of a surprise attack is far greater than if you were aware.

There is no difference between the conscious and sub-conscious states of awareness within life; they are different methods life uses to communicate with its body. Dreams mean something; if you dream of a dog you get to call your own… perhaps you want a dog. It's that simple, there's no higher meaning or some weird fate thing. Life's separation didn't come until advanced species began eating meat and you had Yin (Good) herbivores verses Yang (Bad) carnivores. The battle for higher intelligence is the next saga in this book where I explain as life progressed and began reasoning at a geometrical rate and resources becoming limited, it began the battle between plant and meat eaters to balance life again.

Yin versus Yang

This will explore more into intelligence and reasoning within nature and explain the uses life had for it. The difference between nature verses nurture, yin verses yang is life's ability to use logic against emotion. Herbivores process emotion before logical from their needs in finding good sources of foods to eat based on feelings. Carnivores on the other hand, used logical reasoning to develop better tactics hunting and finding prey to eat which herbivores were always behind in this adaptation race. From self-awareness spawned incredible diversity and a complexity in life started outgrowing the oceans and began walking on land. From high oxygen levels, allowed life to grow to unbelievable sizes, and this section will go into how a certain reptile was almost smarter than primates and life's incredible adaptations to horrific events.

At least on this planet, life's diversity is owed to the ever changing environment earth has slung at it. From ice cores dug deep in the arctic regions, we are able to peer into earths past environments. Giant meteors, huge volcanic eruptions, extreme temperature shifts and tectonic plate movements; earth was anything but stable or constant for very long. By connecting paleontology and geology shows why biology evolved so much diversity. The first cellular species, bacteria, were perfect in stability and reproduction, leading to overpopulation consuming all the resources needed for its survival, but horrible in defending the suns lethal rays. As life became more complex and plants began appearing they thrived from its ability to take those lethal sun rays, use it to break down pre-built molecules releasing electrons and converting it to energy, allowing them to thrive across the globe and introduced different materials in reproducing, causing diversity. Still in shallow waters with resources becoming scarce and limited space life, following the rules of balance, evolved plant eating species to control the population saving the resources. This creates the balance we've known as calling the circle of life. As sense's developed more complexity used in finding and eating plants, it began the predator/prey categories used to balance all the resources earth had.

Throughout history in comparing the species of predator to the prey, the predator is always the more advanced one but unfortunately always the last to evolve. Herbivores, a fear driven creature, were the first by evolving better defenses against the environments instability and advancing movements used to locate or extract the resources needed for its survival. With its ability to reproduce multiple times quickly, gave the species an overall advantage by withstanding the changing environmental factors. Also carried a disadvantage to, by consuming all the resources too fast, it would run out of food rather quickly. This caused carnivores, a content driven creature, to evolve from herbivores with more complex senses and methods used in hunting prey to survive. Which, in response, the prey would evolve better defenses to survive its environment. This made predators, again, evolve better methods in a constant circle to out- smart the competition. This foundation derives from the same rules of balance all matter follows and the survival instinct all life is bound to. Another thing all life shares is the need for similar species to group together, ensuring proper replication. This goes from the genetic structure all the way up to social groups displayed from insects to mammals.

Our ancient ancestor's mammals actually began during the last of the dinosaur era and were the result of Earth's cooling climate. Tiny compared to their predecessors, they developed smaller from the reductions in oxygen levels. As life evolved from the sea and walked onto land, their environment was much like the sea, warm and moist but the air was saturated with oxygen. Before land animals, plants dominated the landscape converting CO_2 to oxygen for millions of years. This single event caused the only time in earth's history where the O_2 levels was higher than N_2, CO_2 or any other element. This did a number of things like created the Ozone layer as O_2 was energized by solar radiation bombardment, allowing for an additional oxygen atom to bond making O_3, earth's ozone. With this lack of CO_2 it caused the most devastating effect, basically suffocating all the plants with oxygen and the result came from the oceans when animals started walking on land. Is it just me or does nature seam to repeat in patterns of cycles based off changing variables, improving itself to adapt environmentally and survive? That is the definition of evolution by the way.

Towards the end of the Cretaceous period something interesting was happening to a certain type of species, the Raptor. As the planet started cooling naturally food became less scares as dinosaurs didn't like cold regions and left. Hunting as carnivores became challenging for new methods were needed for the changing times. This made the Raptor who hunted in groups, begin evolving by remembering. They began reasoning on a level never achieved before on earth from forcing themselves to recall repeated actions and repeat them over. This lead to language by designating certain sounds to mean specific things like food or help. Creating a very primitive social structure for the Raptors and gave personalities to them from increased memories. Competition for females paved way for competition between males and endurance, strength and intelligence were tested. Plant-eaters were no good to test on, they weren't even considered work for they were far too easy for the Raptor… they needed a challenge… they needed to hunt a hunter.

       As carnivores evolved in complexity the everyday things they did would develop more complex as well. The primary function they and all life does every day is eat so their methods on acquiring this would increase first, ensuring their survival. This was seen in primates evolution as they developed the spear first in order to better acquire food. Something different from us to a carnivore thou, we didn't originally kill things in order to eat but they did. Hunting for them is easy and turns into a game of competition against themselves. Humans had to work at hunting for millions of years before we were the top predator on earth. The Raptor on earth began hunting bigger carnivores in a game against one another, testing them. At least these competitions lead to a benefit and propelled this species light years ahead of mammals, chimps or humans for that matter. There's no real way to tell exactly how advanced they may of gotten but one thing is for sure, had it not been for the devastating asteroid from a major event in our solar system the Raptor… not mammals… would of dominated this world today. Evidence found dinosaurs had already begun developing feathers before the asteroid hit and the planet froze. This suggested the origin of mammals from the late dinosaur era in colder regions where it was needed to regulate their own body temperatures. Feathers would lead to fur and the ability for herbivores to generate their own body heat by insulating it. This was natures response to the slow cooling of the planet, life was adapting. It is interesting to see adaptation work especially in this process, cold produces a nervous response to inflame and surge with pools of blood in tiny spots, goose-bumps. Before the end of the cold blooded era from life emerging from the oceans, it began insulating itself and getting to colder regions… it was almost too late. If the asteroid had hit any earlier life would of regressed back to the oceans and started over again for the 3-4th time, at this point who's counting anymore? Just look at geology about how "stable" our planet actually is not, it is quite funny. After the collision, life fell hard and everywhere was ash, frozen wastelands…this was hell on earth.

The asteroid that nearly wiped out all life 65 million years ago, I believe did far more damage than we think. Not only did it shatter the crust and penetrate the mantle but the shock wave echoed around the planet and ricocheted back; this shock wave is what did the most damage to our planet when it hit, think of an egg squeezed till the shell cracks. Massive volcanic eruptions worldwide, entire oceans vaporized or so polluted life struggled to survive, a blanket of deflecting debris plunging temperatures for millions of years, dramatically increasing the speed of the continents and altered the weather in a spin of ups and downs that has lasted since then to this very day. The days of warm, moist highly oxygenated consistency were over and life's cushioning was now a fight for survival. The two main species that managed through earth's darkest days, since the formation of the moon, were the Mammals and the Aves. Both coming from the land of the large, these two developed smaller and used resources less. The Aves, developed from the dinosaurs as small scavengers, originally flew kind of like a flying squirrel but later developed feathers instead of fur. Still laid eggs but was warm blooded, their diets were simple in a world of nothing, worms. The second and final one of the complex species, the mammal, was one of hiding.

The mammals were developing during the late Cretaceous period, right before the dinosaurs were annihilated. Small and always hiding they stayed out of sight for they were tasty treats to the dinosaurs but after them there were no predators, anywhere. Sure the world was in a nuclear winter but around the equator it still was warm, anyone left headed there. The mammals for millions of years, just like the dinosaurs, evolved bigger as the world got over its little cold sniffles. These animals were land crawlers with extensions built for running and climbing. Covered in fur they mostly lived underground or in bunker type houses and over the years they stayed in the jungles but one species began living in the trees. These species were special, very special for they were the ones where we came from, the Simian. Both ape and chimp derived from this one species that began living outside their usual means and one in particular paved the way for the Rise of Primates.

Rise of Primates

In this section I'll explain the evolution of our species from the dawn of mammals to the ancient primates of the land apes and the tree chimps. I will show why certain groups evolved, while others didn't. What made Africa so unique when, compared to other species across the world, humans happen to come from there... and became this ultimate super predator able to dominate all other species to the point of extinction. However there is a concept that must be understood first before you'll see how this all happened, Northern Africa and Saudi Arabia were not always deserts.

Both originated from around the same time period, the late dinosaur eras, but unlike the dinosaurs both were able to maintain their own body temperatures. In a world of ice and darkness with little oxygen and food, it made the warm animal's king above the reptiles dependency of the environments stability. During this time period known as the Mesozoic Era, one group of mammal herbivores thrived in the deep jungles across the world... the Simians. These mammals were unique by developing extensions on their arms and legs to use for grabbing tree limbs and escaping any predator with ease. This surplus led to the group of Simians splitting into two separate types, the first were the larger of the two and lived on the ground – the apes. The second was the more agile and lived in the trees – the chimps.

These mammals existed back when Africa and Saudi Arabia looked much different than they do now and is the reason why only a certain group of chimps evolved into primates. Africa's desert wasn't always so massive, true there were parts towards the central regions that were becoming deserts but much of Africa's northern half was flat, grassland type. A temperate area, it would make Kansas look like Jersey. There was a mountain region right smack in the middle that was once filled with life. As a matter of fact, much of the northern regions of Africa were very different than it is now. Just like Saudi Arabia, in its northern regions as well, were much like Africa's fertile dry grasslands much like modern day Turkey but much of its southern regions resembled southern India or southeastern Asia. Logically it you look at the "eastern half" of the planet and follow the equator, everywhere by a water source is lush in vegetation... except Saudi and Africa... why? The Red Sea and its two gulfs, Aqaba and Suez, were not there. Let me say again... between Africa and Saudi Arabia a long time ago there wasn't any seas or deserts, there was a lush valley protected by mountains next to the ocean, technically the Gulf of Aden. This valley surrounded by mountains was our Eden, where the Red Sea is now and what happened to it is something of great tragedy.

However, apes and chimps were herbivores that lived in jungles not flat valleys planting gardens and building towns. Eden's valley wouldn't have been of interest for us until we learned to grow crops. 2 million years ago we just barely learned how to poke an animal with a sharp object a bunch of times until it stops moving. Planting fields of crops to produce our food and allowing us to remain in one spot was not on our agendas. How we evolved from chimps and none others, well first is a lie, there were others who did but they have all been interbreed or died out long ago. No other regions in the world has massive grasslands right next to lush jungles except Africa and is why primate evolution occurred only there... allow me to explain.

The general theory is tree dwelling primates lost their jungles due to environmental changes and lived in grasslands causing them to be scavengers and evolve. I believed it as well but couldn't explain why we didn't go back south to the jungles and why were we so desperate to start scavenging. My problem was I didn't take into account the 2nd species that existed alongside of us during that time, the great Apes. After the dinosaurs, there were not many predators and in the jungles of Africa there emerged a herbivore that adapted to the thick trees as safety and food. However this species split into two groups, the tree climbing chimps (smaller, more agile) and the ground walking apes (bigger and stronger). Looking at apes today, their behavior is very aggressive and very territorial. We know from psychology each species holds unique behavior patterns tied to that species and doesn't change much. Apes aggression of today tells us how they would act similar back then as well. Chimps, same thing, they act paranoid and scared and would have been bullied by the apes. All of the sudden it hit me that humans didn't evolve because our environment changed. We were driven into the grasslands from the ape's territorial behavior and forced out of the jungles to live in the grasslands. This was huge because finally it gave an understanding of what caused us to become scavengers in a foreign environment that prevented us from going back to the jungles.

This is how it happened; chimps in the African jungles were having some problems. The Great Apes of the middle to southern African regions were surging northward from overpopulation and limited resources. In an ecosystem that is unbalanced, back to natures rules of balance, will adapt to survive and evolve predators from prey. Predators are the result of life's attempt to balance itself. As a group of herbivores with no natural predators will multiply like crazy and eventually consume every resource around. Life begins to adapt by stressing and desperately finds an answer turning a herbivore into a carnivore, well technically cannibals. These warriors would start hunting their own species and anything else smaller, including us. The chimps were smaller and weaker than the apes and were the focus of the apes rage. We were driven north or slaughtered where we did nothing to them and were killed without remorse. What was so bad about it was the ape's viciousness; guerilla warfare is quite brutal as it is without warning and over just as quick. Instead of waiting around to be killed most of the chimps went north towards the grasslands. In there they were more agile then the apes and able to hide easily making the apes frustrated and finally give up, returning to the jungles. Funny enough, it seems the movie "The Planet of the Apes" is far off key.

Meet your ancestor, a "trigger happy" monkey left to die and became masters of the grasslands who believes the world is out to get them. We became masters of the grasslands, becoming the ultimate predator, until one day when we crossed that line between killing for survival and killing for pleasure, murder. By chance probably these hunting chimps ran into the great apes of the jungles. Obviously this time when ape and chimp met things were a tad different leading to one of the bloodiest wars humanity ever endured of pure murder, the Great Simian War.

Great Simian War

This section will go into the human desire to kill. You see after we were left for dead in the middle of the grass and emerged a super predator, we wanted retribution. During my studies of migration patterns of primates I noticed that we made a "U" shape from western Africa to southern Africa (around Zimbabwe) then east-northeast to Ethiopia…interesting, I thought… Why? Out of Ethiopia we went north to Egypt… why did we go around our elbow to get to our ass?? We could have gone straight to Egypt from where we were, the only thing that was in the jungles of Africa's interior was the Apes. Out of the grasslands into the jungles came a vengeance so determined, so enraged that it slaughtered everything it touched in those jungles.

As we developed as primates, we got the taste for blood and we liked it a lot. We started becoming confident in the grasslands and in ourselves as a herbivore turned predator. We started testing our abilities by traveling further, tracking the food, planning… attacking and winning. We became supreme in killing and surviving and we showed it by inventing murder when we started killing for practice. When a cub is learning to kill, their parents cripple a prey and let them learn to kill something to survive. We would do the same as to become better hunters for, back in the grasslands, hunting wasn't something we just knew how to do. We acquired this technology by going against our natural instinct to just find a banana and some bugs in the trees to choosing to kill an animal, there's a slight difference in reasoning there… This behavior completely changed our attitudes from peaceful herbivores that wouldn't hurt a fly; to vicious killing omnivores pissed off that we got picked on a lot as weakling little tree huggers.

By beginning to hunt and eat meat this surged our bodies with different chemicals and mentalities causing a genetic mutation in our reasoning, just like all the other species of life has done in the past… present… and future. It will do this to adapt when it's forced to either sink or swim and life must choose to survive. The building of muscle tissue in our brains was a result of us stressing our minds to its limits by forcing ourselves to remember. By constantly stimulating it, just like any other muscle, the brain rips and tears then by pumping it with protein it's used to regenerate muscle tissue bigger in order to compensate able to better take the stress. With our new technology needed for survival, this required us to stress our minds forcefully to remember more information to become better hunters.

When primates were forced to live in the grasslands, like the prairie dog, we started standing upright to better adapt to our environment. When we did this it freed our upper hands and, unlike the prairie dog, allowed our hands to use tools much like in the trees. By pure hunger, we started eating leftovers from carnivore's meals. By thinking if they eat and like it to survive, why couldn't we do it too?... so we tried ... and we liked it.. a LOT. Different from a vegetarian diet, meat is harder to process in the body and gives a sense of being fuller longer than just a plain plant diet. Since we discovered meat that, not only filled us up but was all the sudden everywhere, was perfect. Problem was scavenging meant relying on others to provide the kill for us then going for the leftovers while dodging the predators... but that meant waiting... and starving, again. We watched carnivores and how they killed using their teeth to tear the animal's flesh. The key was we needed something strong and sharp that would tear through the skin. Probably by accident a primate was climbing rocks, fell on a jagged edged rock, cutting themselves, possibly died or was at least injured, and we found our key. The knife was our first true weapon we would use to hunt for game, waiting and surprising or chasing them down we attempted to be predators. Problem with it was it required close combat which, when hunting a woolly mammoth, proved to be inefficient especially if defending against predators that could still kill us. Lots of lives were lost during this because our tactics were... well basically... garbage - non-existent. What we needed was communication to coordinate attacks but advancements in hunting wouldn't come until later when we made better weapons.

Funny enough the first tool man created that actually worked looked and was used exactly like the tools we used to get those tasty, nasty bugs. By chipping off a rock to an edged point that mimics a carnivores tooth almost exactly, wrapping it to the end of a stick, with grass gave our species an absolute, first ever, wonder of the world... the spear. this was the turning point that turned humanity from a scared, weak, little prey... to nature's ultimate predator unmatched by and species, to date, on this planet. This simple leap, putting different things of simple purpose but together using them they performed complex actions, is what our genes did as they evolved which i mention earlier. This spear allowed us to attack w/o close combat and increased our chances of a vital attack and surviving. Even with the spear we weren't hunters yet but more like curious scavengers. The one main advantage these walking chimps had over all others was their ability to communicate with each other. Back in the grasslands, sneaking up on prey was rather hard especially if your prey is 20 feet tall like a mammoth. Coordinated attacks were the only way to bring down big game because, other than the scavengers, there were no animals big enough to feed two let alone 15 or 2000.

As we got more curious from hunting simple creatures, we needed a challenge so we hunted the hunters. This was when we started enjoying killing because it gave a sense of control for the first time in our existence which for us was huge. See up until then, primates were kicked around and bullied by pretty much every creature around us. This could of happened a handful of ways but somehow our attention got focused on the jungles. Perhaps a group could have been gathering berries and gotten attacked by an ape; an altercation over food maybe; displaying territorial boundaries which were crossed; or plainly sweet old fashioned revenge… who knows but what we do know is we were very, very pissed off at them. So much that we nearly wiped them out of Africa in a matter of years. This next part is kind of… bad… I'm just warning you.

We do not train to be merciful for only the worthless deserve mercy. In the jungles of war there is no prisoners, something confronts you they are your enemy, enemies deserve no mercy but eradication for we do not train to be merciful… We are the Saipan super predators. As we marched into the jungles we overwhelmed the apes as we were not looked at as a threat. Just some scared little… until they saw us ripping their hearts onto the ground while still beating. We tore through them with our spears slashing and ripping flesh like it was fun. We returned organized, armed and smarter… even the strongest of the apes didn't have the slightest of chances. Scalping their entire bodies, slicing body parts and wearing them as trophies we went blood drunk. Don't think that this was limited to just men either; women and children were slaughtered or worse. Rape isn't something that happened when we became civilized, it's been going on forever and though out all species. I saw on The Discovery Channel once this male bat rape a female who clearly didn't want it. That wasn't the saddest part though, it was her child right there who saw the whole thing and couldn't do a damn thing except watch. Can you imagine the emotional shockwaves this would cause? Babies and children just executed, left to die or eaten. If we had a meat eating diet and we were in the middle of a war, we couldn't just stop to go hunting for a deer. We would eat the meat already slaughtered… the apes; It wasn't really cannibalism but pretty damn close to it. We destroyed them and there wasn't much left after we were through. It was probably the bloodiest war our species ever had the pleasure of performing.

During the war, it was too easy slaughtering the apes. The chimps that emerged in Ethiopia from that war were different than the ones going into it in West Africa. They were meaner, emotionless – almost like they went insane with rage, just came in and took over the place but keep in mind too that they were pushed out of the jungles, we just returned the favor. There was one group, Erectus, that proved to be the one sole survivor but their journey was no sweet lullaby, was no stroll in the part. It was so intense, so challenging that had they not done it, instead of indoor plumbing, we would be picking leaves and digging a hole in the ground still. As you will see through Erectus Epic Odyssey, Erectus and Neanderthals were the only ones left standing and they produced, over a series of events and small adaptations, humans of today.

Erectus Epic Odyssey

Arising victorious from the simian war came one hominoid species Homo-Erectus, our ancient ancestors. In this section I'll follow this primate's insane journey north and out of Africa as the world's first super predator. To the north in the European, Eurasian and the Middle East regions; To the east and to the Asian, Indian and Pacific Islands these hunting chimps were very intelligent for their time. However, they were not the only smart chimps, there were a lot more than just one. In order of progression the gentlemen that gave this world humanity were Hails, Gautengensis, Erectus, Ergaster, Antecessor, Heidelbergensis, Heidelbergensis, Cepranensis, , Neanderthalensis, Rhodesiensis and finally Sapiens. These are your elder's ladies and gentlemen, respect them for they've earned it; they've done more for us than we ever knew. To the primates, thank you we owe everything to you, if no one will say it than I will. It's hard to believe people who say we didn't evolve from chimps when they consider someone with a different tan not even the same species. Now let me show you walking, talking chimps exactly where you came from and at the end... I'll show you our Eden.

By learning how to hunt together in packs from the war with the apes gave hunting more structure and making it far more efficient. Causing a surplus of food which would spoil or attract other predators, storing food was needed to keep unused food safe to consume another day and hidden. This would lead to constructing containers to store them in an effort to make transporting food easier as we migrated greater distances to follow game. More importantly with storing food, we could hunt bigger game and not have to hunt every day just to eat helping ensure our survival some more. We started making tools specifically for construction, moving away from tools used for weapons and began engineering which advanced us into the agriculture revolution. From the wheel we learned that round objects are the most stable shapes because when pressure is applied it is transferred evenly across the entire structure. As a matter of fact the "Arch" developed by the Greeks was not new, it was old technology from the wheel just used in a different way much like our development of spears. This reasoning, along with construction and our desire to shield us from the elements, lead to building round huts made from large sticks in a cone shape wrapped in animal skins. Huts were made to quickly takedown and put up to follow game easier and made surviving the ever changing climates a whole lot better.

The main advantage Erectus had over others was the development of the larynx or vocal cords. Back with the apes... well nature in general, especially during mating... sounds of confidence thru feelings arose the most attention from others. Therefore the ability to speak was highly needed with primates, not just for mating but when hunting the apes we needed coordination so again we forced ourselves to keep trying to make different sounds than what we already could. You see people today don't really understand how evolution actually happens, life must choose to adapt or die... it's that simple. I can give hundreds of examples of species that have become extinct and others who have survived due to their incredible adaption, like the crocodile, the best one by far is the dog. Dogs were not here before humans, there were wolfs. Over the centuries, we have bred them to specific task from the bloodhounds in England to the big displays of power in China, the Shar-Pei. If we didn't need to hunt or remember an animal's weakness to kill them tomorrow, then the surge in protein would have built our arms or legs, like the carnivores, not our brains. So to clarify our evolution into humans wasn't from sum freak genetic mutation or by a plant-eater all the sudden eating meat, it was because we chose to, it's that simple. Again, Darwin and Sagan were right, thank you gentlemen. Maybe one day we'll grow up.

I can without a doubt see behavior similarities between chimps and humans where there need for attention, dominance, love grooming each other, their constant panic type demeanor, their love for banana's, how they both will lounge in the shade all day and snack not doing anything, their excellent tree climbing abilities, their eyes and how expressive they are or how fearful and loving they can be and how about the most obvious one – they look exactly like us. Put it this way, we don't look like no zebra we are chimps and they are humans. Homo-Erectus was one of the chimp-like primates (2.3MYA) who could speak simply, walk upright and use tools able to construct spears, huts and containers for food... the perfect migrator. At first they were natures marvel as the first super-predator able to hunt the hunters. Now there were several waves of human like species migrating out of Africa but unlike Erectus couldn't communicate as well. There were however 2 distinct waves of Erectus out of Africa, the first hit Spain, Eurasia, India and then back to Africa. The second wave hit the same places Eurasia, China this time and not Spain but Europe.

Rising from Ethiopia, north towards Egypt, a large group of these primates began following game. Some stayed but many went away from the region and north along the Nile. Perhaps it was the bloodshed from the war drove that drove them away; possibly technological, social or intellectual indifferences. Once at Egypt they split and went 2 ways; one was headed for Spain and the Europeans, the others went toward Turkey. The Turkey bound ones got to around Iraq, northern areas of Saudi Arabia and split again curving around the Caspian Sea and headed towards India and the others toward Eurasia. This journey would have been rather pleasant as it wasn't a desert and had plenty of shade, warm temps and enough hunting to last the entire way. The only way I can come up with on why Erectus kept splitting up, again I was not there personally, seeing how we would react in a similar situation. One reason could be taste, certain animals stick to certain emigrational paths and it's possible they were following animals. Another could have been a difference in leadership or direction. Another could be terrain or they could of hated one another or there was a theory I had going with some convincing evidence where the splits were due to technological advancements like clothes or storage containers or even the beginnings of cultural differences.

To get in their heads, all you have to do is put yourself in their shoes... so to speak... how would you perceive it? When you understand they are us and we are them, I promise, you will understand them and maybe yourself a little more too. Now the European bound ones went across Africa's northern coast. Before Eden flooded, the landscape looked completely different. For example, Greece completely connected to Turkey, the black sea wasn't there, Spain and Sicilia was connected to Africa, North Africa and Saudi Arabia wasn't always a desert and is the reason for Erectus migrating out of Africa and how they got into Spain. Crossing into Spain (2-1.8MYA) from Africa's northern tip of Tangier-Tetouan they went into Spain and the heart of Europe settling in the caves. At first they flourished and loved it deep in the mountains as it had everything they needed to survive – shelter, foods, fresh water. This is probably why their craniums never grew much past Erectus, for in the mountains, the need to keep advancing was gone. The only problem with their new found paradise is they went in it at the wrong time. The earth had been on a warming trend as they and Erectus emerged from Africa before plunging right back into an ice age. In Spain and the Europeans the cavemen became trapped from being too settled and the intense cold. By the time the ice age hit hard, most of the cavemen were becoming isolated in families who were dying out from inbreeding and disease. There was a small group that was able to get into Italy and far enough south to survive 1.5mya. This group is the ones that mixed later with Neanderthals but the ones in Europe, cannibalism took them. As food ran out they started turning on the old and little ones first, then eating each other.

These two separate but similar species were the first migration wave out of Africa but they weren't equipped to survive the toll massive migrations have on a species. As displayed in elephants, intelligent species that migrate over long areas require social interactions and support to cope with loss of other members, wrong turns, the feelings of loneliness and an environment set out to kill them around every corner. Our species that migrated out in the first wave did not posse these vital skills, for language was invented back in Ethiopia. There was a group of Erectus I believe went back to Africa for a while to say. What emerged during the second wave was different, the Heidelbergensis but what made them so much better at migrating than the first one wasn't really as easy as I had though, again not much evidence. Let's say your following game and migrating, you sleep and the guy standing watch is asleep in the morning... where did the game go? Hominoids were good at thinking but not smelling, there was another scavenger that we looked at as our brethren, the wolf. This concept was missing the whole time, that's what made us good migrators; from our mutual benefits working together man and wolf formed a single entity connection that to this very day can be felt. As humans would migrate they would need guidance and companionship from an obedient tool, the dog. The second wave that came from Africa had with them dogs and for the first time they didn't have to find food anymore, our dogs did it for us. This allowed us to venture into regions we could not before and would wind up in some interesting places.

Now the Erectus in Eurasia went all over the place from Russia to China to Indonesia to even to the America's. One certain group stayed in Eurasia and became slender and a faster runner from the openness of that region. This group in the Eurasian area developed a rather neat little trick that made them unique above all other primates. As storage for food became a way of life, pottery began as a means to transport fruits and veggies back to camp. As we would pick through them we would throw out the seeds. As this group of primates migrated with its prey, as animals would migrate in circles, they eventually came back to the same spots year after year. Until one day, they noticed some plants growing where they had discarded the seeds. All of the sudden we learned the seeds we'd been throwing away actually can grow the plant from which it came from. We started using pots for growing the plants and ensured our survival. This gave rise to agriculture.

Another group Erectus went across the bridge north of the Red Sea that connected Africa to Eurasia, some however went into Europe. Perhaps through Turkey or perhaps they crossed from Africa directly to Italy. Whatever the path, they dominated the European regions for many years. The European Erectus, Cepranensis and later Neanderthals, had spread across Europe throughout all its mountain regions developing large muscles and thick bones. Its most impressive advantages were short and stocky body types for strength and conserving heat and energy, enlarged nostrils for breathing in higher altitudes with limited oxygen improving endurance and making a few coed's live together in different groups all in one region created the first structures of families. This passed on to the Neanderthals when they met the descendants of Antecessor somehow was still in Southern Italy. Being the best survivalist of the coldest of regions, they developed a unique technology by trapping animals later called domestication.

Both had mastered their areas with supreme reasoning and adaptability, thou, were not worth anything outside their environments. For example, when they were forced from Europe and would struggle to adapt and survive. What made these species, once the same now so different, cross paths after thousands of years of separation was an event several thousand miles away in Indonesia. A super volcano so massive erupted and blanketed the earth in a darkness causing the northern climates to freeze quickly and making the equator the only warm spot left on earth. This was the event that led these two species flee south and meet up probably south of Turkey. One had agriculture, the other had domestication and combined together in that journey back to Africa found a valley so lush and perfect for crops and domestication. A valley we called home for hundreds of thousands of years and it was the Fall of Eden that started this all, everything we know and have recorded, civilization.

𝕱𝖆𝖑𝖑 𝖔𝖋 𝕰𝖉𝖊𝖓

Most people don't believe me when I say I found Eden, until I show them. They thought I didn't believe in the bible, I don't but I wasn't looking for Eden. I was studying migration patterns of Hominoids throughout Africa, Saudi Arabia and Eurasia when I noticed something rather interesting... so I dug a little. Again, science isn't gaining the right answers... its asking the right questions. Originally I had thought Eden was the black sea because it too was a valley along the coast that got flooded but it was nowhere near Ethiopia... but... the Red Sea is. It hit me hard, the whole time people were looking for Eden on land and never under water. Mosses, Noah and Adam in Christianity are 3 separate stories separated by many years but what if they were together? All over the world there are ancient stories of massive floods or lush beginnings. What I have found is more evidence that Eden was flooded than I need and I still can't believe no one has ever put this together. Let me tell you where our "Eden" actually was and what it looked like.

Eden was a rich and diverse valley between Africa and Saudi Arabia as large as the entire 13 New England colonies. From their two plates pulling away from each other, it sunk the region and stretched it flat to create a bowl shaped dome much like New Orleans. We can view how it would look and act by viewing similar types of valleys between two tectonic plates like for example the California Central Valley. Very similar in shape and climate we can now understand how this Eden had such beautiful weather, several rivers, tons of game, fruits and trees but what made it a paradise for humans wasn't all of that. It was the consistent weather and flat lands for growing crops and domestication of animals. From my own personal extensive studies on this region and others like it, I have found some interesting things. The entrance to Eden was at the northwestern corner where the mountain range barrier that circled all around it was the lowest. This barrier is what kept us from reaching the valley out of Ethiopia that first time we migrated out of Africa. It's possible we turned south at Sinai into the valley but we didn't know how to grow crops or any kind of domestication and relied heavily on the migrations of large animals for food. See Eden had diverse climate zones, much like California's valley, where it was a mixture of sub-tropical type grasslands to arid deserts much like Egypt. Unlike California thou, the climate zones were flipped making the bottom part of Eden very lush and the top part a desert. This would discourage migrating inward and stick to the coastal regions. There was a river, I believe, that was flowing out just like the Nile and it is possible they both connected at one point. Even today you can see evidence on top of the mountains circling the Red Sea ancient rivers that poured off and flowed through Eden giving it fresh water. It is interesting to note that in valleys like Eden and California the ground can get cold while warm air is pressed onto it... thereby causing what is known as Tule fog, a thick layer of fog usually lasting for days until turbulence disturbs it enough to dissipate. Probably just a coincidence, right my Vatican historians?

    No one has ever really thought where exactly our social structure came from. Landowners and laborers have been the two main types of structured society organized since history started being recorded. This was a system originating from two different groups separated by intelligence and used to organize production. The concept derived from owning lands for crop growing and the labor involved in its production. With Erectus (agriculture of foods) primarily smarter but weaker than the Neanderthals (domestication of animals) superior strength and less intelligence they worked together in one location. This is what gave way to the Stone-Age's agricultural revolution. As these two settled the valley, peaceful at first, it quickly became a fierce fight for superiority with weapons of technology. Both had developed primitive sounds used for communication but the alphabet bridged the gap that allowed two races to coexist. Groups of permanent settlements began popping up all over Eden as stone workings and tribal huts merged. Lands were claimed shaping the first social structures with language becoming more complex as some of these settlements grew leading to the dawn of culture. Culture began dividing settlements based on laws and perspectives on organizing production routines changed. This would cause rivalries between cultures and the hunter was reinvented into the warrior.

    War broke out in Eden between societies over land and resources. The organizing principle of any civilization is its ability for war and production's key to military readiness. This led to the noble class designed to show a warriors status and with nobility came land ownership where labors were allowed to work their lands for a small portion. There were complications with war, first the loss of men in the labor class and resources needed proved too costly to maintain. Landowners began interbreeding forcefully with labors crossing their bloodlines together to rebuild their forces and supplies. Culture began morphing into a warlord's worst nightmare and ruled with a heavy hand and that's when things got real bad. Rebellion broke out and the labor class took over everything, interbreeding until the two species were one super hominoid species. The Saipan Virus began spreading throughout Eden smarter and stronger than any primate in its wake leading to the formation of the first human empire starting the Bronze Age. Civilization was on the rise, dominating everywhere it touched and this new weapon of technology was used in the slaughter of all other lesser primates. There was just one small problem, a force outside our understandings at that time had been building for centuries and was about to break from the stress. Completely unknown to Eden, on the other side of the southern mountain range there was a disaster of epic proportions just waiting to happen. At that time sea levels were low but increasing and as the earth warmed, raising the sea levels, the only thing separating our valley from the sea was a few rocks. Extending from the Sana'a/Yemen to Djibouti/Ethiopia region, this kept the rising sea levels from flooding and submerging the area we called Eden and home for hundreds of thousands of years... until one day. When the ground split apart and opened the gates of Hell on earth, literally. As Africa and Saudi Arabia pulled away from each other, forming the valley, it would stretch out the land pretty far until it would snap. Only this snap, was unlike anything ever seen before. To get a glimpse of its devastation, Eden was about the distance between Florida to Albany, New York; the earthquake ripped a tear In the middle so massive that in some spots it was the width of Delaware, others spots about the width of Florida's panhandle.

   This incredible force tore a giant rip right in the middle... of our Eden and was about the size as the state of New Jersey. Being a witness to these events, seeing the ground just open up and fire and lava pouring out killing and burning everything it touches, would defiantly give me a concept of Hell and its characteristics of just how real it was. As horrible as that event was too happened, it still wasn't the primary blow to our species that nearly killed all of us. Between Djibouti (Africa) and Sana'a (Saudi Arabia) there was a mountain range that connected these two areas together. What's left is now called "The Gate of Greif" that is a little piece extending into the Red Sea at the mouth of it. From what I can tell, it didn't just crack the dam, the quake shifted the entire continent of Saudi Arabia. This was devastating as the pressure from the Gulf of Aden got so strong that I believe it blew the mountains apart. Standing there it would look much like a dam just shattering apart and all you see left is a 200-300 foot wall of water coming right for you... what do you do? The breach was massive. Evidence that I can see ripped apart Djibouti where the wall of water first hit and then flowed two ways (southwest and north) eventually draining southeast into Somalia. In the heart of Ethiopia there are mountains that appear of been carved out in a southwestern flow of water that's dotted with lakes and rivers along the way and appears to of drained thru the middle of Kenya and going south into the Indian ocean.

The water surged northward, hitting Africa around Asmera (north of Ethiopia) and hit the mountains there with such force it blew chunks off them and breached thru Eritrea. Then like a pinball went back and forth hitting Africa then Saudi Arabia until it straighten out and headed right for Mount Sinai. When it hit Sinai it parted (Hey, just like Mosses) going NW and NE towards the mouth of the Nile and Jerusalem, curving around the mountain making Sinai an island in an entirely flooded world. From the NW surge into Africa caused massive devastation to the northern regions that were once fertile grasslands but has turned it into the desert we know today. I have found more evidence that this has happened than I ever wanted. First, the lines in Saudi Arabia... Has anyone ever wondered how curved red lines that looked like water flowing downward, curving around mountains, actually came from?? The chunks of huge rocks just sitting in the pathway of these lines, they look exactly like the missing mountain tops from the southern coastal regions of the Red Sea where the water blasted them off. How about the large salt pan in the middle of the Sahara desert, where a pool of salt water sat and evaporated leaving the minerals? Along the coast you can also see water lines on the mountains as to suggest the pathway this flood took into the heart of Africa. The indention to the west of the Nile almost looks like a 2nd delta. The line along the mountain range going from the southern tip of Sinai, northwest, towards the Mediterranean Sea and to the opposite side in Africa, west of Hurghada, the exact same line going in the exact same direction as to suggest... a large body of water surged through there and what's left is the Gulf of Suez... Or how about the volcanoes I found in the middle of the rip under the Red Sea as to suggest that the rip under the sea is a giant fisher saved by the massive flooding that sealed it. Had that not happened, it would have made the Indonesia super volcano look like the ones in Hawaii.

Next was Saudi Arabia, it received the worst blow. As the water surge curved around Sinai it also headed northeast towards Aqaba (southern tip of Israel). However, the elevations in Sinai and Israel are higher than in Saudi Arabia and pushed it south where it breached at several points from

Aqaba to Tafilah in Jordan's northern borders next to Israel. You can clearly see the water pathways in Saudi Arabia heading south towards Riyadh, curving towards Yemen and east where it pooled north of Oman. As a result, much of Saudi Arabia was under water. The same boulders found in the middle of the Sahara, are also found in Saudi's desert. Even at the southern tip of the Red Sea where there's a peninsula off Saudi Arabia's southwestern corner that the ancient's called "The Gate of Grief" shows us that something massive happened here. During Sapiens migrations out of Africa, of the 3 groups, the ones in Yemen migrated south along Saudi's southern coastal areas. At first I thought this was for food but it wasn't, Saudi Arabia was under water and they had to stay south. In Sinai, being trapped on a mountain top that is surrounded by water, would give the illusion the world was under water and would be where the story of Noah came from. Also some nut job that'd gone crazy by the utter devastation he witnessed, mixed with the lack of oxygen and food, would make him hear voices and claim they were gods.

In Christianity Adam, Noah and Moses happened in 3 separate events over time... realistically they happened at the same time, the same event. This is why throughout the globe, across multiple cultures, there is some sort of paradise beginning and a massive flood story. Moses is unique to the northern group because of their perception being trapped on a mountain but all of them shared one major thing in common. They each thought they were the only survivors because after the waters receded, there was nothing left... anywhere. This event is a once in a billion shot occurrence that is extremely rare and very powerful. The loss of life was severe and the quickness of it is horrific part, no one had time to react. Once the flood killed most of us off, what mutated from this was a virus so potent that anywhere it went infected it with The Sapient Virus. However, in the long run the flood actually saved us because it neutralized the quake that was so massive it would have plunged the world into another nuclear winter after just coming out of one from the super volcano in Indonesia.

𝕿𝖍𝖊 𝕾𝖆𝖕𝖎𝖊𝖓𝖙 𝖁𝖎𝖗𝖚𝖘

To classify humans or any other species, aside from physically, behavior is also used in observing their lifestyles in classifying who and what they are. They're analyzed, separated by birth, rate of growth, body structure, environmental adaptations, and their consumption of resources, reproduction methods and death. When applied to our species, humans are similar to mammals but in fact not, for they are the only ones who consume beyond their limits. Every animal in nature and on this planet is part of a circle within its environment in order to maintain stability and survival for all species. Humans however will go to a location and devoir every natural resource until the only way to survive is spreading to a new location. The only other species on this planet that can be classified the same way, a virus… yes agent Smith was right.

Eden's devastating effects is what shaped our cultural differences. Our population went from 10's of millions to a few thousand in minutes, wiping out our existence like it meant nothing. The survivors started grouping together along the northern, eastern and western coastal areas of the Red Sea but each one was separated from one another by the sea and had no idea of the other groups. Because each group thought they were the only survivors of Eden's tragedy, gave us the 3 main diversified cultures in humanity that to this day still has. Each group had advantages and disadvantages unique to their environmental regions and I'll show you how each one shaped their culture and is what gave us such diversity existing today. Before each group began their epic migrations, they stayed close to their refugee areas for a long time until the waters went down. The massive loss of life that occurred and how quickly it all happened is what made it so tragic. For around a hundred thousand or so years we lived in an environment that was constant and allowed us to thrive in record numbers. As stated in earlier chapters, herbivores w/o natural predators will multiply fast and over populate. Our species got comfortable to the idea that we controlled this world and our fates and no other force was in control. That idea, almost wiped us completely out… good thing primates had such a great ability to climb. Unfortunately set our evolution back about a million to 500,000 years. Again interpreted wrong, humans demise from Eden was not from the fruits from a knowledge tree… the effects of humanity believing their new ways of life using logic made them invincible to any threats or actions to them. Try to put yourself in their shoes for a moment. Your whole world, your reality was doing things unnaturally by trying to be smarter than the carnivores. Intelligence for our species and dominating any threats to our survival made humanity more arrogant.

When our home was just wiped out and killed almost everyone you ever knew in the blink of an eye, which you had no control over, something humanity had a very hard time swallowing and accepting that we had total control of our choices but zero for our environment. Showing us this would break anyone's spirit because you simply don't understand... or... would it be... "Won't" understand... there's quite a difference there between don't and won't. This slaughter Eden provided us, made us believe intelligence should be discouraged in order to prevent another one of gods wraths. The first, (please note, first, isn't referencing time), Western/African group wound up all along the coast and conjugated around the city Eritrea. By far the African group endured the most loss of life with very few survivors. Their escape from the flood was horrible from the limited coastal lands and the difficulty getting to them from the lower elevation. Also the short time they had being so close to the breach caused them to have zero time to react at all to save them or anyone. Most of them didn't even know what had killed them because it happened so fast and they were dead before they could rationalize it. Regardless of that, their supreme advantage they had over the other 2 was access to their home region. Where they could go into the jungles of their heritage and survive without evolving any further. With the moist warm climate, endless food source and adequate shelter, the Western group was setup nice. This is why to this very day humans in Africa still live in huts, hunt with spears and never really moved much past the stone-age. Eventually migrating further south, from Ethiopia to south African region, they were already confident on how to survive. Their reasoning however, was one where they stayed in "limbo" and didn't progress much, from their acceptances of ignorance it helped them to rationalize Eden's fall lead to more comfortable livings and the need for advancing intelligence/reasoning was not needed.

While the Western group had things pretty much set up for them, the Eastern group's environment and migration patterns, had a much harsher and unforgiving course. Their path took them across the southern coast of Saudi Arabia, into India, across Chinas massive mountains, right to Japan, and split north (Russia/Americas) and south (Indonesia/Australia) and the difference they had was perception. Logic was key to surviving environmental tragedies. Since being in the middle of the desert and away from all of our known methods of survival made them evolve different ideas and views on their Eden's destruction. Hunting land animals, their primary means of food, was non-existent in the desert, which, lead to their only source of survival was the ocean. Remarkable to point out, the very same force that devastated humans, the eastern group overcame any fears and actually mastered surviving off water completely. However fishing was completely different from hunting land animals, as they found, and made them rethink on how to catch food. Primitive forms, still displayed and used today, of fishing was standing in one spot motionless with a spear waiting for a fish to graze by and us stabbing it. Also this made them patient and respectful of each other for fishing with 500 as opposed to 1 would catch more food and the need for cooperation was vital forcing them to advance their communications. Patience had led to their mild manors teaching them not to disturb their surroundings by becoming one with their environments.

Also the Asian culture got their high taste for fish and rice because of their migrations was along the coastal regions and why most of them sought out that type of environments which led them to eventually settle Japan, Australia and the rest of the pacific south-west islands. This group was not done and when they reached Japan. They split going towards Russia and Australia, from the lower sea levels, making it possible for them to reach New Guinea and America by land bridges, covered by water now, connecting continents together. This allowed humans to find and spread to the remaining parts of the world. These events are displayed in their religion by their very deeply connected and respectful manner for nature and its processes. This is the core reasoning behind the religious interpretations of the Asian culture of chaos & order, yen & yang and life/death. Through their causes and effects within nature, gave them control of their fates and put them at a higher enlightenment of understanding than any other culture in any part of the world throughout history. This was their primary advantage the Eastern/Asian group had over the other 2 humanoid groups. Giving them their concepts of acquiring knowledge while remaining balanced in their environment and how logic, however impressive it may be, should be led by wisdom in reasoning. Acquiring inner peace was by calming your thoughts, controlling your emotions and respecting your environment. This is where honor comes from and over time achieved wisdom, which aside from logic, was felt logical reasoning where choices aren't influenced by arrogance and supreme to all other perception was equal and should not be favored over the other is what's made them the most advanced and longest cultural perceptive in the history of the world.

Now the 3rd group, the Northern/Euro-Arab one, was the most spiritual of the three but wasn't their advantage. They were the only group who had more survivors than the other 2 combined. The East/West groups were hit the hardest from their placement basically at ground zero. When the flood hit, they had little to no time to react as opposed to the northern group that saw the water approaching and was able to safety get to higher ground better. This is also where the story of Moses and the 10 commandments came from. During the flood, one man went up into the high altitudes of Mt. Sinai, much higher than all the others, as the waters approached the northern region, splitting around the mountain, it would appear that everything, everywhere was flooded and gone. Scared and alone he desperately tried to comprehend why he just saw so much death and destruction of reality… then a violent storm came and brought with it a lot of lightning and wind and what was perceived to have been, God. Panicked now and scared so badly, something very interesting started happening to this human. The whole time he's been higher in elevation he's been suffocating slowly from the lack of oxygen getting to his brain. If someone is freaked out they are usually taking deep fast breaths and with the lack of oxygen would cause them to start hallucinating, making him see and hear voices. From his sub-conscious rationalizing reality by accepting it was humanity that did something wrong and caused Eden's fall, he was able to comprehend which helped validate his reasoning. Trying to analyze the "evilness" and causing a supernatural being to punish us wasn't too hard. By just thinking what the issues an omnivorous species would have by if confined to a limited area and over populating them, you'll see exactly where these 10 commandments came from.

To maintain control supremely, the controlled must think they are less than the one controlling. By regulating intelligence and giving answers to complex questions like purpose and origin, the controlled never asked questions and just did what they were told. I'm getting ahead of myself; I'll explain exactly how religious cults control their follower in the Religious Industrial Complex section. For now let's just say Eden lacked that concept of control because everyone followed their own rules based on what they felt was right or wrong. So… the first 3 rules validated God as the supreme one and thereby eliminating all other "false gods". This made god's words, law and banded humans together under a single perception of good and evil. The rest were in conjunction with the issues described in the previous chapter of Eden's fall where murder, rape and stealing were a way of life amongst humans. By respecting your neighbor and elders, you look out for each other and in turn helped unify us... or at least we would like to think that's the benefit. Honoring mom's and dad's for their abilities to procreate... and they call me crazy even though they believe in talking snakes and magic. So imagine your entire world was just wiped out in minutes and you wind up with some other people, you've never met before, by a mountain that appears to be the only dry land mass left in the world. Powerful storms hammer the area, lightening, hurricane force winds... the dam world is ripping itself apart right in front of your eyes. All of the sudden, things calm and coming down from the mountain was a guy claiming "God" had just spoken to him telling him humans messed up pretty bad and had to be punished for it. In order to keep on the good side, were written rules he had etched into stone... what else would you believe other than a Religious Industrial Complex? Everyone else believed in it and thought of it as true, the one common cultural trait the Northern/Euro-Arab group shared

Religious Industrial Complex

This chapter is one of the hardest to realize because no one likes to be told they've been manipulated or lied to by someone they trusted... What I'm about to tell you is really hard to hear and is something the kings and nobles have known since the conception of the human race, religion was a tool designed to bring order out of chaos. From Eden's separation of the smart from the dumb came the landowners and the labors but with that brought the rebellion from the loss of power knowledge had brought to the labor classes. Paganism gave power back to the landowners by proclaiming them higher and more powerful from gods favoring them over the labors. Even in some cultures like the Persians their religion proclaimed them as god-kings or gods of flesh who ruled the earth with unlimited power. Religion is humanities ancient attempts in explaining the events outside of their current understandings. Things like environmental objects or changes, our creation, purpose and mortality... but most importantly our feelings of perceptional influences were represented by gods of specialty. These gods were powerful and played very important roles in how the universe worked and formed. This important concept of the gods made Paganism favor the royalty and noble classes while on the backs of the labor classes. Throughout the history of civilization there has been to types of humans, leaders and labors. I had always wondered how Rome went from Zeus to the Roman Catholic Church because, between the two, they were so different. When I watched "The Da Vinci Code" and it mentioned the Council of Nicaea I didn't believe it at first. I couldn't believe I never heard of this especially coming from such a deep catholic background, I thought I knew everything about it. The bible never mentioned this Council thing nor did I ever hear of it at church. Was this Hollywood crap or their some truth to this Nicaea, so I looked it up and found something I didn't want to and know why the church tried so hard to be forgotten.

I am sorry if you have never heard this before and are the first time for it was hurtful to read, even for me. The bible didn't fall out of the sky into someone's lap one day but was written by a pagan to regain control of his labor class and his empire... now let me explain. The labor classes has always outnumbered the landowners and in some cases led to them overtaking the rich and powerful. What sparked the one god revolution began in Egypt's labor classes with Judaism. Preaching a single god and prophesying a messiah, it taught equality in all men from ancient scriptures of men on mountains, massive floods and a lushes lost garden. The Egyptians were harsh thou and would not allow a slave to have any rights or privileges as to gain some sort of confidence, keeping them in line. Greece was the first civilization to promote equality in everyone but what changed the world was the formation of Roman senate and having elected officials represent the common man or laborer equal to the kings. This was the confidence Egypt had tried preventing and is what led to the fall of paganism when a new religion gave hope back to the labor class.

At first, this one god religion was mocked and laughed at by the Pagans. This only fueled the fire and caused the labor class to believe in equality even more thereby revolting against their leaders. Rome at that time had expanded well beyond their means and the borders were being threatened by rebels on becoming overrun. In those borders grew a religious uprising in the labor class and started spreading throughout Roman Empire. In the 300's AD, before the rebellion got so bad, efforts were made to secretly crush this uprising by orders placed to kill these leaders who preached of a one god and messiah. Their assassination attempts on the conspirators only made martyrs of some and sent the rest into hiding, fueling their campaign and having the opposite effects hoped for. Officials went "missing", landowners were dying and fear began spreading amongst the nobles so they went to their king in need of a plan to control this before it got to the point of destroying Rome and most certainly death for all of them.

By the 320's the labor class was in full revolt and had reached the emperors steps where people were toppling statues and burning buildings in Rome. The emperor at the time faced a realization most wished had never encountered. If his labor class stopped working, who would build the streets, repair the homes, grow the food or fight the wars? Rome's emperor, Constantine, was no fool for he knew that if he didn't do something dramatic then he would lose his empire so he eventually sent out letters bearing the emperor's seal to the leaders of this proclaimed religion holding these scriptures to one unified safe place and put together a collection of these stories, the problem was getting them there after all the attempts on their lives. This seal meant guaranteed safe passage by order of the emperor himself to, from and during this official meeting by personally attending. This was monumental for this religion as monotheism had never been recognized as a true religion in the history of humanity. In 325AD, in the Hellenic city of

Nicaea, emperor Constantine of Rome held the first Council to write a bible in one of the most heavily guarded city's in Asia Minor as to promote safety and assurance they would be left alone. Provided with security and necessities, Constantine and the sec leaders locked the doors and didn't come out till they all had agreed on which text would go in and which wouldn't. This argument or intense debate lasted for days and was in jeopardy of not being completed. In the New Testament no one could seem to agree on one key figure in the Christian and Catholic religions, Jesus.

Throughout my entire research I had always focused on the Old Testament, I knew it wasn't right but the new one I always protected because I believed in Jesus. When a movie suggested Jesus was an astrological reference to the seasons, I didn't believe it; when it suggested there were other messiah's born on Dec 25th of a virgin, followed by 3 kings towards the star in the east, performed miracles like healing the sick or water to wine, was crucified and resurrected... before Jesus... then I started to believe it and what I found blew my mind, why this is so important is what made sense of it all. Meet Horus of Egypt, Attis of Greece and Mithras of Persia... all born on December 25th of a virgin with 3 kings and a star in the east, who performed miracles and eventually was crucified and resurrected. Jesus had older siblings... or did this guy Peter actually have something viable in his movie? As it turns out he was right but the reason is what makes it undeniable. As Homo-Sapiens emerged from Eden as expert farmers, the need to calculate the seasons were vital for agriculture... but how do you do that, how do you make a calendar? Keep in mind, this is before telescopes, the realization of earths wobble and oval shaped revolution around the sun was unknown at that time. How would you know the amount of days in a year without some sort of reference point? Groups of stars do appear during certain times throughout the year but the increase/decrease speeds the earth has going towards and away from the sun would cause the constellations not to appear on the same day but just a little different year to year. That's because an earth year is 365.24 days long, not really exact, from the oval revolution, which is where we get leap year to make up for the (-0.24 days * 4 years = -0.96 days behind an actual year) lost time accumulated. How do we know this?? As it turns out there is a certain astrological event that occurs in the northern hemisphere when the earth is at its slowest point of revolution moving away and begins heading towards the sun. In the northern hemisphere, where most civilizations thrived, between August and December the sun goes from direct to indirect and gives the environment different seasons. On December 22th the sun stops moving south and suspends for 3 days, then... on December 25th the sun rises north and 3 stars in Orion's belt line directly up with the star in the east and points to where the sun rises and thus giving us our reference point. From there we counted 365 split up into 4-3 month periods. This is what built our calendar long before the invention of the telescope, how else did you think the ancients knew how long an earth year was?

The messiah's of almost all major religions (Jesus, Horus, and Mithras) throughout history was our representations marking the end of winter and beginning of warmer seasons. Did the son of an all-powerful, higher entity actually exist... no, I'm sorry... did a man live who was more like Gandhi and was hung on a cross like all other non-pagans believers or criminals against their system, who knows but it is possible. Could a god-man turn water into wine or cast demons out of a person to cure them, of let's say cancer... No. Jesus, just like the others, was designed to show the labor class that no matter how noble a man can get on earth, their soul in the eyes of a creator, is judged equally to the common man. However, there still was a problem... with Judaism their messiah was to come and free them of being poor and weak to a promise land where they were kings and lived a comfortable life forever. Constantine designed Jesus to have already come but the labor class was still poor and not in a promise land living lavishly... this is where sin came into play.

As it was designed, a human today is born in sin from an action done by the first humans to walk the earth. These two, male and female, were lured by a talking snake into eating an apple from a tree made of knowledge. Upon eating the fruit, instantly they knew of pain and sadness that would carry on with all of their children till the end of time and prevent their connection to the creator. Jesus wasn't there to free the labor class, he was there to allow humanity a connection to the creator again... he just had to die willingly first as to deter seeking vengeance on those who killed him. This is the clever part of Christianity; equality is achieved only when labor is produced under the preset guidelines consistently until death occurs, not by their own hands, will they be judged on where they spend eternity... clever... even if it isn't true, at least they worked without resistance. The system that emerged from Nicaea worked like a charm and by showing his support Constantine was baptized. Rome became unified again, resistance dropped almost immediately and it started growing stronger for the first time in a while, but it was short lived. In the east grew two iconic figures, Mohammad and Buda, who taught similar perspectives on a one ultimate god. Having many more followers than the smaller and much newer Jesus messiah the eastern religions made its progression very difficult after the fall of Rome, until England and the Vatican. For the next 2000 or so years the Catholic and Vatican's wreaked havoc all across Europe and almost to Japan citing all who oppose as enemies of their god and must be cleansed. In response to this imbalanced outbreak another organization caused Their Secret War to begin behind the scenes as to control not by force but willingly enslavement of themselves through debt.

Their Secret War

In this chapter I'll show how this war is a result of good karma and how the Christians deserve every bit for what they've done throughout their existence was far worse. I discovered this by peering into the life of Germany in the 20th century. I wondered; Hitler, Stalin and Japan hated the "free world" so much that obviously... since our system and world today isn't working... their point of view was at very least analyzable to check if there was any validity. History would say Nazi's hated any other race except Arian's and didn't like the Jew's very much... why? What was his problem with a certain religion that he would single out them and not any other one, like Japan's, at all?? So I watched the videos of his speeches and I have to say I was inspired, not for the 3rd whatever or Germany but to give the control of the country back to the people who are a part of its future. Turns out Hitler had no problem with religion, at all. I listen to his speeches, he doesn't mention religion as an enemy, and he mentions bankers as their enemy and needed to be overthrown to take back control of Germany to its people.

Wait a second... that didn't make sense until I learned of Germany's state after World War 1. As part of their treaty, Germany owed more money in restitution to the world that it was impossible to repay and rebuild their nation at the same time. Bankers of England and mostly America approached Germany to loan them money to do all of that, only thing was the interest rate keeping them in debt and making the bankers rich and owning things from the utility systems to the schools to the government. One banker in particular, J.P. Morgan, was head of the loan committee to Germany and during the 1920's attempted to restructure the loan to get Germany to repay it back... which they weren't. In the summer of 1929 their last attempt went rather bad and Germany basically told them to shove it and they weren't paying them back. Now this caused a problem because Germany could not be touched, due to the treaty and Morgan went back to America insulted and enraged with no forcible recourse... except his buddy's idea, the one in the oil industry.

JD Rockefeller had systematically tested the markets a few years earlier in 1907 causing a panic when he told people the banks were out of money, causing a run on banks making banks start calling in loans to cover the loss... crashing the system by freezing credit... and creating the need for the Federal Reserve Act of 1913. This was a part of the plan to get a centralized banking system installed in America. During the 20's credit was expanded 100 fold and the world indulged after a world war nearly destroyed everyone. When Morgan who greatly financed Rockefeller's operations came to him for a solution to Germany's rebellious attitude, they came up with the idea to seriously crash the system again. This would cause two things, call in the loans to destroy Germany and stress America into accepting a central banking system. In the same year Germany told Morgan to piss off, in October '29 him and JD quietly pulled out of the markets and crashed the system hard, causing the great depression, freezing credit, destroying Germany and leading America to the Federal Reserve System in the 30's.

This is what fueled Hitler's Germany by starvation and desperation and lead to him taking control so easily and why the German people followed him so blindly and fiercely. They took control of their utilities, public buildings and resources from the banking system, destroying all of those who operated them. Anyone would do this to any foreign occupying organization by force providing opportunity for their family to survive by eliminating wealth's classification system used since humans began using wisdom-reasoning instead of fear-violent tactics to create and maintain control of the nobles labor class's to build a king/ god-king/emperor/pharaoh's personal kingdom. Beautiful societies were built in the past from its lower poverty labor class by manipulating and controlling the rules for credit and profit goaled. Societies such as Rome, Egypt, Persia, England even America used this system to build monumental achievements used to show their level of control and size… and in the past, those empires in addition to India, Germany, Russia, Korea, Cuba, etc. resisted that control were no different from George Washington's motivators used to support his battered soldiers during America's revolutionary war against England.

So what was with Jews and banks? Why is it when we say someone is a "Jew" they don't share with anyone? Exploring this turned up one name, Rothschild. This family alone is what started the banking system we know and use today so I explored into them and since they were very secretive, it was hard to get any clue to motives or origins except fragments which actually in the end gave it away. I asked, "Where would a Jew from the ghetto (Poor Jewish community) get the idea, motivation and $20,000 to start a banking system designed to put people into debt"… in the 1700's? To understand this I had to look at Jew's and their past. Since its formation, Judaism has been downed and crucified by every single religion that interacted with them. Jew's were slaves in a world of Paganism which favored the rich and elite. Jew's prophesized a messiah that would lead them out of chains and into the promise lands... he never came. As stated in the previous chapter, Christianity surged in Rome causing a rebellion to leverage the construction of their bible and ensuring its survival by turning Rome from Pagans to Christians almost overnight to save a dying empire. Constantine wasn't stupid as he designed the church to serve him by enslaving the labor class through debt, by gaining more taxes, while providing them false hopes of equality after they used their lives as servants to the nobles and kings before they died.

The Knights Templar originated as the guards from the Council of Nicaea who knew the church was used for control not redemption but at first they went along with it because it brought so much happiness to their people, the lower class. Until the fall of Rome... then things got complicated. Christianity needed a new home and England was the strongest in Europe and was without religion unlike Eurasia which was thick in their religion and would have destroyed them for they were much more powerful in the east. Once in England spawned the Vatican, a group of high priest whose sole purpose was the elimination of all other religions to give Christians world power to free humanity of the disordered differences in our understandings. A king in England, James, rewrote the bible to suit him and charged these "Holy Knights of Nicaea" to spread Christianity to the world so all may have a chance of redemption from oppressive god-kings or emperors.

The Crusades was successful in two ways; one is it gave the Vatican unlimited power and two it showed the knights returning home religions real motives. This caused the Knights and Vatican's relationship to degrade which the church couldn't force their silence, since the Knights were war hero's and had enough pull with the people to cause a revolt. So the Vatican paid them, heavily, to keep their silence. Despite their attempts and disturbed by their motives with very rich lifestyles, the Knight's created an institution that would give out large sums of money and sometimes charge a fee or percentage on top of what was borrowed. This allowed the Knights to play chess with the world powers by funding operations designed on completing an alternative task. The Knights thru 1200 AD – late 1300's began recruiting helpers to run this new system causing things to happen in the world. One plan was the fall of England by getting their enemies to attack them in an attempt to break the Vatican's power in Europe. One plan involving France failed and was blamed on the Knights as manipulators and deceivers. The Vatican knew they could no longer control the Templars compassion and drew a plan to fix that problem. Personal orders from the pope himself were sent out secretly to be opened at once on a certain day, Friday the 13th. These godly requests were instructions to kill all members of the Knights Templars including men women and children, seizing all their assets and proclaiming them manipulators of Satanic motives, releasers of evil ways and devils in the flesh aimed on destroying the church. It worked like a charm except one tiny issue, some escaped and were presumed dead with their mother lode of riches thought to of been found.

In a world full of Christians and proclaimed as Satan worshipers, the Knights who survived their slaughter had only one place the Vatican would never think to look for them… the ghetto and the Jews finally had their messiah who would lead them out of chains. The Knights married, had children and taught the Jewish people the truths of the Christian order and gave them a system designed to control a society by funding its enemies while empowering them by interest. After a few thousands of years of torment torcher and misery from the world, the Jews finally had a way to bring their people out of slavery and into prosperity. Finally giving them the chance to preserve their culture and not be afraid of persecution from others. In the 1700's, emerging from the ghetto, they began their plan by sending one to Germany called Rothschild with 20 grand and starting the central banking system the Templars used. In a world that was expanding rapidly, credit was needed to ensure each cultures desire to survive and be supreme amongst all others… spreading the banking system worldwide to the system we know and embrace today. This is where the Jew's got the idea, capitol and motivation that began and built the banks we use today. Unlike the beginnings of Rothschild, the system grew beyond their control when it was no longer restricted to their family alone which caused problems when one would go renegaded, destroying a society. An institution was needed to regulate while ensuring the spread of its banks across the world, thus the IMF was born. Enslaving the Christian world by promoting credit and capitalism while fighting communism, for their banks failed in that society by government controlled businesses, not banks has lead the Jewish people out of chains and slavery. It also made Jews actually liars for their savior did come, gave them a tool they used to rise above the ashes and brought honor back to their people. Compared to The Scientific Revolution, no religion stood a chance when it hit the Info Age though.

The Scientific Revolution

"To ensure our long term survival, we must search the stars. Let's hope we can only last until then." – Stephen Hawkins

Carl Sagan I believe put it best when he referenced the universe, in all its wonder and marvel, to be not as glamorous or complex as we want it to be. That it's actually simpler and less mystic than what religion tries to sell us and we are able to comprehend how and why it works. This is my problem with religion, lack of knowledge in the labor class. That knowledge is for the privileged, loved and civilized individuals and shouldn't be shared with poor, pathetic and incompetent less minded individuals for it's used for the illusion that landowners have ownership and superiority over the laborers in order to maintain structure for a society. For redundancy, something was needed to offset the imbalance in lifestyles between the two classes and religion was born. To control knowledge, advanced reasoning like afterlife, destiny and creation along with purpose was explained with vivid stories and moving motivational speeches to mask the truth, bringing a sense of unity and empowerment to anyone who believes. Feelings are manipulated from the expressions of importance in believing, unquestionably without seeking and creating faith.

Faith is not really a word it's a method of reasoning where emotion is used despite logic. That proof is not required to the believer for comprehension of the design, purpose and origin was not needed for their cooperation in providing labor to the elite for all will be judged after death of course. Knowledge was meant for the ones who processed abstract thoughts a lot faster than the other slower ones (who were ignorant wastes of life anyways and will never amount to anything) and above all requirements for intelligence, the more civilized were always the firsts in line despite arrival. Clever, I must say, because anyone who would challenge religions reasoning or knowledge were opposed, quickly suppressed and met with anger in disrupting the system. Why else would prison be the best recruiting ground for faith, it's perfect. Someone acts out against the structures religion has provided, met with opposition and anger then quickly suppressed forcefully and their left all alone to believe perhaps they were wrong. Well since you're a product of your environment, good and bad, then society would be at fault for allowing things to get so bad... for remember... only the privileged deserve prosperity and the rest have a blind eye turned to them, well as long as society has redundancy in its labor. Fred went to jail which is tragic, his life and production stops, no big deal. For meet Paul, who is just like Fred and don't know or care about the last guys position he's replacing so willingly. Now labor can continue again, whew, and finally the tragedy is over for production is starting again… now… who was Fred again? Just some guy who messed up? No one cares what happened to him? Perhaps he'll come out saved or "rehabilitated" or if not… he'll go right back for more education until he is. As I've said before, clever… real clever until a thinker named Isaac Newton.

It was believed long ago that man was meant to stay on the ground with the serpents in a life of pain and misery from tying to achieve knowledge from a tree back in Eden. If man was meant to fly, he'd been given wings therefore it was God who kept us on the ground and unable to soar in the clouds with him until a life of servitude and death takes us. Isaac had noticed when fruit would fall from a tree it would always hit the ground at the same time. He had an idea that this force was constant and measurable despite an objects weight. Privately he knew that it wasn't God keeping things on the ground; there was an outside force manipulating and moving the objects pushing them down which could be calculated saying "What goes up, must come down". He measured the time it took for different objects to hit the ground and that's when he proved to himself he was right. Despite weight an object always fell at 32ft/s, ALWAYS, meaning a battle axe and piece of coal would hit the ground at the same time when released at the same time and therefore if you propelled faster than 32ft/s then would you go up and not down.

This was a problem for the structures of society as it questioned the knowledge of religion, it would threaten their control by allowing the simple commenter to reason if one part is wrong in the bible then what else would be? See knowledge was for the powerful ones enough to handle the effects of abstract thoughts. Free thinking is what broke down society before by radicals rebelling against their leaders of power from the unbalance nobility brought against laborers. However Newton felt differently as the universe started seeming less and less scarier and mystic. For him, the perception of existence was more practical and people could comprehend new knowledge and it could be useful, not harmful. From this observation, Isaac and his family almost lost their lives as the church lashed out hard. His evidence was undeniable and the church eventually gave in by claiming "Interpretational errors".

Before Newton, nature and science was viewed as magical and untouchable by man. This evolution in humans, science, evolved from the need for technology and medicines, mostly meds thou. However the church viewed science as demonically influenced and claimed many times people of this trade as heretics of the Holy Lands. At the time our concepts of the world was much different like the classic example of the compass. Ship building was imperative and ship captains were told not to venture very far... you might just fall off the planet... which might be bad, I guess? Anyways, as the need for technology increased, so did the science behind it and it began picking at the bible. Those throughout history who've advanced humanity thru scientific means were only wanted when it was important, the rest of the time they were nut jobs or even demonic. These people gave their lives to better humanity and were not interested in fame or fortune, simply just for the truth. They were slaughtered emotionally, sometimes physically for wanting to learn by experimentation.

Charles Darwin (The, Evolutionist), Nikola Tesla (Electrical Physics Engineer), Albert Einstein (Atoms and Fission), Georg Ohm (Resistance in Ohm's Law), Stephen Hawkins (Astronomer), Isaac Newton (Gravity in Newton's Law), Barbara McClintock (Geneticist Powerhouse), James Maxwell (Optics), Carl Sagan (Amazing astrophysicist), Plato (Visual Perception), Wegener (Continental drift), Pasteur (Microbes and Disease), finally Semmelweis (Antiseptics) all were some of the best people humanity has ever seen and all risked their lives and their families as well to stand up for the truth against a world who hated them... and it took Aristarchus of Samos, Galileo Galilei, Nicolaus Copernicus and Johannes Kepler to convince everyone that the earth was not the center but was part of a network of planets revolving around a star. It took Edwin Hubble to show the universe did not revolve around the earth and our solar system was actually part of a network of systems revolving together in a hurricane shaped way called the Milky Way galaxy and this "galaxy" was actually part of a network of millions of other galaxies spread out across a universe. These are just to name a few of the one's we all owe are admiration and comfy little lives to, for life would be very different without them, everybody needs to shut up and realize where the fuck we ACTUALLY CAME FROM!! You think we dug up microwaves or energy transfer fell from the sky?

Over the years as I learned who these amazing people were it enraged me to find how the world treated them and tried keeping them down at their levels of, as they say, blind faith. It was claimed that these great men (and women) of science and logic who thought differently were devils of witchcraft or malice set on destroying humanity and everything good and pure. However it could be just me but it seems like making medicines and energy production isn't as evil as we might think. One would perceive what is evil or good based of morals from pleasure verse guilt. The result of an action performed is perceived one of two ways; either it makes them feel good or bad and can manifest into figures that are a representation of them. They need to keep mindful and aware as to follow the guidelines needed for a systematic controlled society. Good and evil are points of view where, depending on location, a group of people's perceptions and lifestyles are similar in manner which reflects how they feel about the world together. So let's venture into that dark realm of the fallen one they call Lucifer, Satan or the devil. These iconic figures, much like their opposites, held high ranks in the battle of good and evil for the souls of mankind. Just mankind thou and not snails or eagles or koala bears either, all of them are just mindless robots I guess...

Regardless of whatever name a society perceives as evil or wrongdoing, its meaning has always been the same, a "crutch". If a person performs an action outside their society's acceptable limits, a common excuse is an evil force had manipulated them into choosing to do wrong. This takes the responsibility away from the individual and allows them to not feel at fault. "The Devil" as it's put in many cultures is in fact real but only thru a person's perceptional manifestations. My best example is disease; let's look at that for a spell, ha-ha... Illness – the result of a pathogen or microbe entity invading, destroying and spreading within a host... or... as religion says an entity of pure hateful energy from another dimension used to influence emotions, controlling a person's choices to destroy everything and get revenge on the one that damn them. The benefit to this reasoning was allowing acceptance to an event outside your control making illness perceived as an un-curable situation; not a result of a pathogen that was invading the body that is CUREABLE. What religion has done is yield reasoning that inspired fear or confusion where obedience was mandatory. By taking the responsibility away from a person and blaming it on an outside force, outside anyone's control, makes us accept there is nothing we can do to stop it, except rely on another outside force to intervene or religion as some call it.

This exists even in today's world with mental disease or demonic possession where our behaviors are explained and blamed on forces outside of our control. This gives an excuse, allowing emotion to dictate reasoning and judgment, making the person a victim of evilness invading their minds and shouldn't be punished but handled delicately. Just like evil, good is used to describe certain behavioral patterns. Everyone and I mean everyone has multiple personalities or as I like to call it... masks. Humans will mask themselves differently based on their environment or social situation they are in at that time. Like the difference between someone at work and home, two completely different people that share the same body. Used for acceptance, each personality is triggered by an event of their choosing which can drastically alter behavior and beliefs almost instantly. This is a defense mechanism to mask their true feelings, weather to adapt for survival, acceptances and attention – or – to deal with a situation that recalls horrible memories and by switching personalities it changes perception and thus allows the situation to be dealt with rationally... well as rational as one over the edge can get.

Well if there is no actual heaven or hell, then something has to happen to you after you die... right? So... how sure are we that there is an afterlife? For years I struggled with this one, trying so desperately to incorporate some higher being into science but I never could and I tried. I would come up with some wild ones too but every time I would break them. Until one day when I stopped fighting it and explored into life after death without god. I didn't want to trust me but to understand the truth I had to give both sides a chance. I couldn't deny the evidence or the logic but the meaning... the meaning was the hardest to swallow, it really was the end. The way I peered into death, without dying first, was to study people as they died. All creatures that die a slow death have one thing in common; before they died they felt tired like they wanted to sleep. So to begin explaining this let's look at sleep and what happens to the body and the purpose for this. First we need to define the difference between the conscious and sub-conscious state, one we rationalize as controlling dreams and the other self-awareness. As explained earlier, the flow of electrons across a series of molecular "switches" yields certain action by manipulating the electrons wave formations. An action brought upon by an electrical charge that is used for molecular reorganization so weather its identifying light or repairing an imbalance in the kidneys, technically each signal controlling and reading are sent from and received in the same way, with the same things. The monkey head switching experiment Stalin attempted, not only showed what a soul was but also where and how it was used as well.

You see death is actually not a part of life; it is the result of life's imperfections. As a body's functions maintains at a normal and constant operation, its cells will divide and breakdown at a similar pace as to regulate the organ without defective cells. During a vital injury, the body goes into a sort of repair mode and the feeling of tiredness comes quickly. This is because energy is being diverted from the senses to the injury by allowing proper allocation thru the nervous system to flow directly and not freely. However when an injury occurs and the loss of cellular tissue is severe the body does something rather interesting, shut down. It stops the flow of all sensory input/output signals and is diverted it to the injury, flooding it with energy. As this happens the injury is preparing for a reproduction fest by stock piling nutrients and destroying the damaged ones to prevent them from multiplying and leading to organ failure. This systematic procedure is imprinted in every cell, in every helix to multiply like crazy when threatened by extinction. Well with taking that and applying it to sleep it says that "sleep" is the bodies way to repair vital organs as to act like it's threatened, every night. Without sleep the only organ that's affected is the brain by recalling and retaining errors and sometimes ocular misinterpretations when comparing real-time signals to memory storage and seeing things that are not there. This realization comes with it a concept, I myself had a real hard time accepting it, there is no afterlife.

I used to think the afterlife was much like a move "What Dreams May Come" with Robin Williams where death was a construct of your memories as to paint a "heaven or hell" for you to live eternally. Researching how memories are stored and retained it was clear after 7 minutes the brain starts deteriorating and data corruption occurs. After that your memories and your soul deteriorates with it but keep in mind that 7 minutes can be a long time dreaming, perceivably. Ghost, demonic possession you ask? There is a fine line between them and multi-personalities and ghost hunters will tell you almost every time, the unexplainable, is explained. The other times, that can't be explained, are times where the factor was not out in the open. Just because something is unexplained at that moment, doesn't mean there's an actual bunny inside a magician's top hat. People see what they want to see and memories can get corrupted. Recent studies on eye witness accounts have shown something rather disturbing, 8/10 times their wrong. The guy had a red hat and blue shirt, some witness swears it was a blue hat and a red shirt – they can see it vividly... Until there's other eye witnesses and memories are challenged on validity.

Reality compared to dreams is sometimes hard to decipher. Let's look at being scared, all senses are maxed out and the brain is reading signals franticly, searching for some sense of reality. Any sudden noise, movements or environment shift (Like temperature drops or gusts of wind) will cause a chain reaction in the brain to find something now so it can stop before it shuts down from over stimulation. During that process, if it doesn't get results, the brain will construct from memory what the eyes want to see by manifesting imageries on top of reality, kind of like Photoshop. What I just said is your brain will make images appear in front of you as real as anything else, one classic example is the mirage of water in the desert... classic. A person is lost in the desert and wants so badly to find water, well the brain is searching with no results until, one moment in desperation they swear success. They start drinking the sand, at first it's the best water ever, then as they swallow and the other senses go off contradicting what we think is real. All of the sudden the water fades and they are left with confusion; we laugh at the crazy thirsty person drinking sand – yet – others tell us there are magical flying men and trees with special fruit, talking snakes, gates to hell in a volcano.. And we don't laugh, we feel it with them. When I was a kid i was walking home from school one day and I wanted to try a new shortcut... well I wound up at this barbwire fence and no other way around except the long way back so I went over it. I made it but I cut the middle of my palm deep, like real deep. Scared my mom would get mad I wrapped it up and it healed fine with a scar. Several years later I was at a Christian worship group and I told them it was a satanic ritual mistake I had done that I wanted to repent. They put holy water on it, I acted like it burned, it didn't but they believed it did, really believed as one claimed they saw smoke. Did they just save me?

As science progresses, so does our understandings of the world, eventually it will replace the knowledge we thought was right. This will lead to bigger problems than we have today. More people today are turning to atheism instead of religion than ever before. The reason is they believe in something, something of higher order, they just know religion isn't it. They don't know why it's wrong, they just know it doesn't make sense anymore since the world is round and they're germs in the air that makes us sick. Unfortunately for religion the truth isn't on their side anymore; science isn't devilish these days... it wasn't really the one burning women for freely thinking. It was only a matter of time for survival to force humanity to learn science. The religions of the world are not ready for this new "Info Age" era for their structures are not solid. It was inevitable for us to find the answers to life's creation but in order to comprehend them we had to first learn how to ask the right questions. The idea a higher power did not create anything does not diminish life's purpose for what's left is the truth where we have earned our right to be here. We realize that we were never placed here for a reason; our reason is because of our determined placements here. What that means is we adapted from situations and events occurring during our evolution from chimps to human and that is special because no other species done this and survived.

   This is what I want people to understand, what all members of science has tried showing; fantasy is not reality, its reality and the things in this universe we do not comprehend doesn't mean we can't understand. Fate is the results from your choices constructing the world we live in and not some blueprint that has no causality or accountability. That is my problem, by believing this reality was given to us, we take no responsibility for our own actions, at all. I've heard people say "Well I'm not going to be around to see it so who cares?" if any of you feel the same, tell the children of this world that instead of trying to make things a better world for them and the future, you just said fuck it and good luck. Humans technically should've been extinct a long time ago and most of them did. The one's that chose to adapt and survive are the ones now trying to destroying themselves. Humanity has become a virus upon itself and to this world. We have infected the oceans, the air, the forest and even ourselves. During darker times in our history religion was used as humanities medicine bringing order out of chaos, making civilizations; turning these scared, battered, confused, hunting walking talking chimps into humans... the first super-predator plaguing the world into destruction but... there is a way to Survive the Epidemic by cleansing our way of thinking.

Surviving the Epidemic

This is about the fall of governmental, religious and social classes and how to avoid it ripping our society apart. Our species has such potential, I see it vividly but our structure for life was designed to fail for it was never meant to prosper, it was meant to maintain. This system would be perfect now if there were unlimited resources but unfortunately this isn't a Mother Goose fairy tale, were not in Eden anymore... this is reality, not fantasy. The 3 major forms of structures used for the regulation of resources and production levels are   - capitalism (individually operated), socialism (partially operated by a government) and communism (totally governmental control). All three of these systems, for a fact, will fail for the simple reason they are all operating on a monetary system. Originally a foreign exchange tool, money would become a type of convenience turned necessity that creates motivation thru debt. In America (And I never knew this) the Federal Reserve is not owned, operated or governed by their government. Thanks to the Federal Reserve Act implemented, coincidently enough, started taking gold for paper currency getting away from the gold standard. This was only done because of the Federal Reserve Act of the 1930's after the 2nd intentional tanking of the markets in October '29 by J.D Rockefether and his good buddy JP Morgan which continued on and again in 1987 and 2008. People have witnessed corporate greediness just take people's lives and throw them away. Can't say i blame them, especially when we see how the military handles their personnel after their no longer useful.

Capitalism, cleverly designed, it uses a method called "Fractional Reserve Banking" where it does exactly what it says. The total amount of reserves a bank has is a smaller percentage, or fraction, than the actual total number of notes circulating. This deflates the value of the notes by making 100 notes have the value of 50. For example, a government borrows money, let's pretend it's the first time and there's no money in existence to start. A bank will loan money at interest so for this example let's say it's a 100 mill... at interest. So what this means is we own the bank 150 million back on a loan we got for 100 million. Tell me, how can you pay 150 million back on a loan for 100 if there is only a 100 million notes in existence? It's an insane hamster wheel going round and round headed nowhere fast with one goal, debt, ultimate debt.

In America it is said everyone can own their own business, well if they all did, who's going to work for them? An old expression my grandmother used was "To many chiefs and not enough Indians." Funny how right she can be from time to time, almost like she's seen a couple of things in her day. Also just as funny; in America the business way of life, the very same system it supports and values so much, is the very same system responsible for the ethics that took all of its jobs. I saw a classic example when America went to the Latino's for its labor. The Americans claimed their unemployment was because of the Latinos taking over their jobs. What's freaking hilarious is the Mexicans weren't the ones going to Home Depot in the morning recruiting them as employees. The Mexican workers are doing what ANY ONE OF US would do to better their family's lives, period. You want to blame someone; blame the ones giving the jobs away cause in America, as the pimping industry would say... don't hate the players; hate the game.

Apparently everyone's been asleep for the last 300 years because American greed has spread globally now... you can thank the Cold War for that so let's examine America for a moment. In its beginnings, it was formed from a bunch of slave owning rebels not wanting to pay their taxes trying to break away from the banking industry in England and promotion of religious values. Who eventually designs a system that implements money as the driving factor; from a Roman structure of government that fell of corruption issues? What floors me is they designed society from this and are surprised when it fails in the exact same manner as before in Rome. I guess they expected the same action would yield different results? And who designed this system?? Oh that's right the businesses...in business, there goals, their motives are not for the betterment of humanity, it's about profits... well say, that's a great idea! Why hasn't anyone thought of... this... before... oh wait, they did that's right and... THEY FAILED! Do I have to spell this out for you? Perhaps we should try a different approach, maybe?? You think that might be logical since society structure hasn't changed since the Stone Age?

We have to start thinking, if we are doing something that is counterproductive and does not better humans then it needs to go. We need systems, societal governess and directional purpose that is productive for the species and not for the individual luxuries of a few. For the ultimate result of that system is one gets all while the entire rest get nothing. Then there's communism which basically is capitalism reversed and government owns the business and just uses the citizens as labor for the betterment of the government. The production value from this is insane, just look at the USSR. After the fall of the Berlin Wall, the world got a glimpse into what Stalin was up to all those years. What was found amazing, within 20 years, they had more tanks, more jets, more nukes at least 50 times over America's stock pile. The black market went insane and that is pretty much how the Middle East grew in power.

  Corporations will become more powerful than the governments they operate in. The fall of the labor class and the re-attempt for control by the corporations will be the worst part of all. As robotics get more advanced and become more efficient they will replace the industrial sector which in turn will take out the commercial sectors as well and all the jobs will fade. As that slowly happens, more people become reliant on their leaders to fix it and take care of them. This will collapse the entire system for the illusion of security we found in money will disappear as the value does. Once the monies values is stripped, social structure and order will crumble almost overnight; panic and confusion from the loss of control will motivate people to do things they wouldn't normally do. This is what people don't realize; it doesn't matter how much paper currencies one has, what matters is in the value of that held currency. That's the goal of a monetary system, collapse by devaluing, through debt a regions resources is stripped of its value and acquired easier. Don't believe me, don't take my word for it just ask Congress where all the gold in Ft. Knox went, The FED took it but they've seem to of misplaced it. Governments will do the same thing and attempt to regain control by force using the military causing civil war. Someone will strike first but by that time war would be the only recourse or way out. The only thing I think that might prevent it would be compassion, if there's any left by then. As cities, states and countries go broke they will break down and at first simple things like road construction or the DMV stops. As it gets worse, things like Medicare or 911 go offline and society breaks down. Even as I write this it seems like desperations going to be first out the door, before it all goes downhill fast. At that moment you will see just how primitive we all really are and how much we act just like chimps.

The most dangerous person in the world is one with nothing to lose; you take away peoples CIS or their nice $6.00 Starbucks cup of coffee and you'll see how quickly people will go crazy. The devices that distract us from actually being logical will soon be stripped and by the time people look up and finally see, it will be too late and society will fail causing fear, confusion and leading to pure anarchy. At that point I believe the red buttons will be pushed and say goodbye to everything because unlike any previous times where civilization has destroyed and remade itself anew, this time we have the power to destroy the world at least 200 times. Before I published this book I was talking to a nuclear engineer about this book's validity and the end came up. He believes we will make it out, very few but humanity will prevail… my friend has more hope for humanity than I he believes compassion will keep the red button pushing party at bay. I disagree for the most dangerous person is one with NOTHING to lose, why not push it? I would, so would over ¾ of you, don't say you wouldn't because if your entire world was stripped from you, without warning and you watched everyone you loved die in pain and agony… you wouldn't push it?? Bullshit to the liars, I know you would to the honest ones

Achieving Humanitarian Maturity

So what's our goal? What's the point of all of existence, to prepare for death? You see the problem I have with our species is we think we are special. That life was given to us for the ability to choose between a bologna or ham sandwich? That this whole universe was constructed simply for us… on the edge of our galaxy in the middle of nowhere… tell me, when are we going to grow up? If an alien race found us, unless they wanted something, they would just keep going claiming humans were too primitive to contact. The idea that the human, and only humans, soul is anything more than electrical signals manipulating molecular shapes is counterproductive. Let me get this straight, we can't cure cancer because we don't want to kill a zygote and take their souls… are you kidding me?? Who came up with this society… oh yeah that's right, we haven't changed social structures since the Stone Age, why stop now since everything's working so well?? It upsets me sometimes when people would make fun of Star Trek and them just flying around. Yes that's exactly what they're doing, just flying around looking at stars… but they have no poverty, no famine, racism, sickness, depression and don't forget they know where they're going to sleep tomorrow. They go to a meaningful job that they love which appreciates them; yes let's laugh at the space freaks that live so weird.

It's not that the world or universe is pointless or not special because some magical being sitting in the clouds didn't go "Poof" and created this perfect design called life from boredom. Have you ever looked at a double helix? Studied paleontology and how species became extinct? Perhaps child birth, people think that's the best way to have offspring? That an appendix in humans is a mere coincidence or our genetic structure matching more with a chimp than a mouse does to a rat. Life is anything but perfect; it's more like a controlled chaos where a series of adaptions, from an energized molecule, yields an evolutionary leap on a genetic level causing the little thing I like to call LIFE. The point, the purpose of all of this is not to achieve some paradise in death but to SURVIVE. Look around you; cells, viruses, bacteria, trees, fish, bears, humans all share one single drive – survival. The fact that we came from no god doesn't mean humans are any less meaningful enough to survive, on the contrary. As shown in earlier chapters, our existence WAS EARNED! Humans have fought hard to get here today and so many tragedies and horrors did we endure. This paints a different picture of humans where we were scared and kicked around to the super predator of today unmatched by any species to date on earth, except one, ourselves.

We go through massive environmental tragedies, horrible climate shifts out of nowhere, battle against social disbarment within our species, fought illness and injury over a span of hundreds of miles over thousands of years... only to give up now and wait for something, ANYTHING that kills society as we know it today? Looking at how we earned our place here should tell us of humanities endurance and strength to survive... it should make us proud to be human, not ashamed. We're displeasing some magical cloud guy? We're displeasing ourselves and were the ones who have to deal with it is us and our children. Molecular dioxide osmosis is how electrons are used to spark chemical reactions that produce reactions that are exerted in a directional set path. Building onto these actions with different ones and you'll get more complex movements... and so on... and so on. Awareness is life's ability to sense the world and souls are constructs of perception, based from the electrical impulses of awareness, and when compared with memory recognition gives us a sense of time.

Social structure and culture derived from the perceptions of what's good and what is evil to bring order from chaos and provided purpose to events outside our control. Our constructs of heaven came from our observance in the sun and rain clouds roles in bringing life back in spring. On the flipside, hell came from Eden when the ground opened up and fire, lava and death came up with a vengeance. Which leaves death, the single most mystery people today hold on to, as their proof something else is out there. They do not want to allow them to perceive a universe that when a soul with character dies, that's it. This scares them and makes me appreciate life so much more for there's only one shot, one chance to live and not just survive. Once you sustain vital injuries enough to stop the heart and you die that's it, 7 minutes and the brain deteriorates and corrupts memories, destroying any essence of you left. Why is it we are so concerned with death? Is it from Eden and the quickness death can come? Perhaps that is why we feel the need to have death's living arrangements secured. I know the world's problems appear so big, so far gone but I refuse to allow it to happen, I can't allow that, I won't... I want mine and everyone's children – humanities future - to be safe. I want us to prosper and If I have to tear apart religion to secure that, than I will. As a matter of fact, I think I just did in this book with my molecular dioxide osmosis.

I was going to build a society in this chapter and show everyone how easy it was but I remembered how much humanity likes the world the way it is. They like the problems, if they didn't I believe they would change it. Changing our world is not about new buildings or better technology; it's about our mental processes and reasoning methods, our drive and our goals. Instead ill show certain key things we can change that will lead to our prosperity from the labor going to robotics, using a non-single leadership, separating children from adults, using skyscrapers as greenhouses, uniting under a single human race, securing our resources to recycling technologies. This will yield to us realizing there is no magic that we control our fate, only then will humans reach maturity. All of the problems we face today are no one's fault but ours and ours alone. People tell me all the time that our current system just needs fixing and repeating the same actions will yield different results. We are not thinking right at all and our priorities are no longer about survival but what satisfies our emotional desires.

See, this world is full of very good observers who comprehends the issues humans are plagued with… however… there is NO ONE who can figure out a better way other than re-using the same system of tools that we know don't work. Our structures of leadership will fail from its individually led direction. That structure leads to the allocation of resources and their purposes for the use and benefits of a few. One thing that will probably be the hardest concept humanity will try to understand is people are important… a person is not. Individuality is the most harmful divider to our race by dividing us into categories or groups of similar perspectives and claiming we are different. This would lead to our need to raise children individually as to maintain that uniqueness by using children as programmed robots of property whose intentions aren't about prosperity of their species. For when they become adults who can be productive, they get a meaningless one to continue the perspectives of not caring about anyone by themselves leading to the breakdown of social structures and interactions. What is humanity's goal? What is it that drives and motivates us? What is the root causes of the problems that threaten us today? What is the point to all of this, our ability to choose and wait for a mythical being of unlimited power to erase his error creating the human race by destroying our existence? Or… are all of our sorrows from our own creations? Are perspectives is the thing that is preventing us from breaking this cycle and really achieving pure tranquility, let me prove it to you by asking you this one little question…

If you could cure the entire world of all diseases forever simply by killing one innocence person, regardless of age, could you kill an innocent person?

Most of you would say no, not because you like illness or like to see people suffer. Our concepts of murder are influenced from the desire to obey an ethically structured set of rules erected from society's perception. Murder is murder, in taking the life of another being there is no difference between a serial killer and a solider besides their cause. Throughout history there are classic examples of murder that has been "justified", especially at the top of the list is our consumption of meat. You want to see murder, go to a slaughterhouse it will make you vomit. Certainty wouldn't be eating a hamburger for dinner that's for sure. Another reason we can't seem to fix the issues of today is because we have people making choices who have no idea what the hell is going on... for example... the President of the United States. Tell me, how exactly can someone adequately be in control of the world's most powerful military, who has NEVER served in the armed forces? Senators making laws governing health and human services, who haven't worked an E.R. shift lasting 36 hours during a full moon in downtown Chicago before.

So how do we fix this shit hole that seems too far gone to repair? I know how but to warn... you won't like it because it requires changing our perspectives. I've divided this into different section touching leadership structure, curing famine, fixing unemployment permanently, perfecting an educational system and getting rid of our desire for personal self-gain. First and foremost, protect the elders as they are the smartest humans we have as age is no number, it's an accomplishment. Those skillful enough to survive, reach a wisdom we only wished we'd be so fortunate enough to have the ability to listen to. Which is probably the most valuable resource humanity has ever had. Any society, regardless the species, requires adequate leadership especially in the more intelligent ones. Leadership is not needed for direction, purpose or ideas, it's the wisdom leadership provides that can unite many as one single life form to complete a common goal. It is wisdom that knows the problems of many outweigh the few and takes responsibility for the actions of the unit and takes no recognition when successful for it takes all as one to achieve perfection. The building of an elder council will provide prosperity by choosing for the betterment of all while excluding their own perceptiveness influencing their judgments in how they're able to unite humanity, from confidence. It is stupid to assume elders are inferior to younger or of no use and not needed in our society. Young and dumb is a dime a dozen but old and wise is priceless and takes a lifetime to achieve. In today's world we have people making important decisions who have no experience or wisdom to even know what they are doing. For example environmental laws are made, not by a geologist, by someone who didn't study for years the effects engineering of the Mississippi did and how it has killed many species in southern Louisiana's delta regions.

Eliminate all mining, service, production, raw manufacturing, transportation, utility, construction, agriculture, waste management, infrastructure security and medical jobs. As well as all banking, investment or any other financial institutions including the stock markets in getting rid of the entire monetary system through the advancements in robotics, matter/energy redistribution and the bioengineering of humans. Within 10 years all of the world's problems will disappear… within 10 years… Insanity… listen, the reason 99% of you hate your jobs, isn't because you don't want to work, its cause your jobs are meaningless and repetitive with no achievable point but retirement then death. What's insane is we seem to repeat the same actions hoping for something to happen and rid us of this insanity… Production value isn't tied to manual labor it's tied to efficiency levels. Logically we don't need laborers anymore and to be quite honest, humans are horrible at those jobs anyways compared to robots. So, to rid our society of the pointless jobs, we automate everything. With robotics they don't get tired or have labor laws, take vacations, get sick, don't need workmen's comp or need maternity leave, they love manual labor. Self-driving cars and planes running on a networked grid eliminating human error, crashes, traffic… robots mining resources and manufacturing raw materials, automate the food and service industries entirely and have machines produce our food supply. Using skyscrapers as food pods completely ran automatically. This simple little concept would turn one sq. acre into 100. Construct medic pod capsules where a person can lay in and is body scanned, diagnosed, cured and if needed performed surgery on and we'll fix the medical industry.

The military is trying to make a mobile pod used to repair a solider wounded on the battle field to return them to duty quicker and ensure hospital type treatment is administered quicker decreasing the death toll. These "med-pods" are able to body scan the patient, accurately diagnose, perform surgery if necessary, treat, cure and release onsite within hours of the incident. What this will do is it will eliminate the dependency on doctors, surgeons, PPO/HMO's and hospitals by taking away the need for labor. Ask any... ANY elder in America today 2013 about the difference between doctors now as opposed to when they were young... see what they say, I dare you. Tell them stem cell research will cure cancer, Alzheimer's, MS and can perfect cloning. If they needed a heart, no problem cause we could grow them one from their own DNA... they could actually run again as if they were teenagers. Bet they say yes and be all for it, not arguing over if it has a soul or not and leading back to the importance of an elder council.

Next, resource control, including inventory allocation based on necessity. Using skyscrapers as large greenhouses and turning 1 acre into 100's would cure famine forever. Completely automated these super greenhouses would yield food all year long in any environment. Advancing the way we use products and making recycling methods able to reuse 100% leaving no waste. Hopefully it will help make us realize matter needs to be used in a cycled type way for if they are not then we will realize real quick these resources won't last forever. To live in space, you must be self-sustaining.

Probably the worst issue and the one single tragedy that, if not corrected, will be the root cause of our downfall... children. Above all else (you, me and anyone old) children are the most important for our survival. Child abuse, foster homes, alternative schools and juvenile hall are the examples we have on treatment for our youth. Before we get further a lot of people have argued that we might be rushing adulthood and irreversibly not allowing them to be children. This reasoning is obsolete for the fact human children take the longest to reach maturity than any other species in the history of earth.

First off, CHILDREN DID NOT ASK TO BE HERE! They are not toys, leverage, punching bags, sexual objects, paychecks, cheap labor... inconvenience's, source of pity, stupid, troubled, lost or incompetent. THEY ARE OUR FUTURE! This treatment of our precious prosperity NEEDS TO STOP IMMEDATILY. Our children's faults, is our failures as their teachers and products of their environments is an adaptation method life uses for survival. Depending on how a species handles their offspring determines their rate of progression. It occurred to me one day that our cultures way of life, referring to our ancient style of living together by genetically similar groups of people called families, has not changed since the Stone Age. Here's the problem; we are born, we grow up and learn, we achieve a degree, finally get a career and then have a family. This system of adults working and raising offspring is a double edged sword. It affects the adults by hindering their production value. Children are affected from the lack of attention and humanities future is compromised, no wonder we're not going anywhere. If we could have children in a controlled environment where they will be safe, educated and mentally stable until adulthood where they can all have a future. This would free up the adults and allow them to produce more research and development. I have ask women about taking raising children away from people and they all have said no way... but then I ask if they have ownership over another human being, that's when the conflict begins. This feeling of ownership is a way we acquire attention or want to pass something down in some despite attempt to hold on to individuality, again guys are we children? Does it matter if little Johnny learns how to fish with his dad, if he can't even go outside from ozone depletion?

Next is space, I suppose a self-sustaining energy source would help but they still want to use lasers to produce fission and waste it by grounding the neutrals then we won't fix it. When instead you could recycle and by sending the neutrals back to the reactor compressed into microwaves sparks plasma... has anyone ever wondered how fission occurs to helium on the sun's surface? Perhaps why we haven't done much in space could be from a lack of energy production? Does anyone know where the electrons come from a generator? Generators use this technique call an EMF, where spinning magnets revolve inside wrapped wires and pull the electrons (static) from the air to a compressed wave form... there's no static in space. The problem with a self-sustaining energy source is it would destroy money, if everyone had free everlasting energy why would they work? To fix that give those meaningful jobs where they feel a part of something while their respected in their field. Bet you they come to work.

Finally dissolve individuality and break the chains that have separated our race based on perspectives and not by species. It is normal to have hobbies or trades that one enjoys but to portray an image of self-recognition as to mask true feelings of perspectives is childish and stupid. If you need society to accept you every day to function then you yourself may have confidence issues that require attention. If you don't think this chapter draws out a society that will prosper, just look around and ask how the current one is working out for you? We will never understand Beyond our Reality until we achieve maturity in our reasoning and understanding of the universe and its wonders is not magic but a simple process from the attraction and repulsion of subatomic particles. So with all the jobs gone and everything automated, what do we do? Simple, again, research and development in advancing our race to prosperity… what else would we do? Destroy ourselves? Perhaps drown in entertainment and false senses of security? We have no choice, well that's not true we do, we have to fix our society before it rips itself apart and I know all of you see it.

Beyond Our Reality

Our race might want to stop trying to find other life out there because we should be careful what we wish for. Through my research into reasoning and predators I found something. In nature it isn't the herbivores that evolve to the dominate species, always it was the carnivores. Advanced predators don't care about our culture, don't care about preserving life. The way I found evidence, besides the obvious, life existed on other worlds was our neighboring planet was Mars. The planet Mars once was able to and contained the first molecules combining together in helix formations... whether or not it officially contained life has no relevance, it had the possibility to and that means something else entirely. If 2 out of 9 planets contain the molecules and conditions used to spawn life then the amount of other life outside our solar system in the entire universe is astronomical. Many people simply don't realize exactly how big the universe and the unreal amount of other galaxies, stars and planets there are. Based on our own solar system, 2/9 = 0.22% of planets are able to contain life... try 10 trillion planets, that's 22% of 10,000,000,000,000 = 2,200,000,000,000 planets containing life or better yet let's get realistic, try 10 trillion clusters (groups of galaxies)... astronomical. AND YES I DID COUNT PLUTO AS A PLANET. See if just a handful of those planets that has life, contain intelligent life, the odds we are alone is not too good.

That's the problem also... through my studies I have found more evidence that on other worlds throughout the universe intelligent life is more and likely to come from carnivores. They are more likely to evolve intelligently, making them the, again, dominate smart carnivores outnumbering the submissive smart herbivores... umm that's us guys. We keep searching for life, I'm not so sure we want to find it or will like what we see. Put it this way, they won't look like any Vulcans or anything close to humanoid. Things in this universe has always seemed magical and beyond our understandings, until we find a better way to look at the world. An example is my theory on energy. It is my belief that gravity is no anomaly it's the opposite of light. For example, they are attracted to each other as seen when light bends towards a black hole. See to understand what light and energy is, you must describe what exactly is it doing. Light is not anti-matter photon whatever, simply it is a proton and an electron together. In order to show you how this happens and where I got it from I give you, "Little Big Boy", the Hydrogen bomb.

Funny enough the field that started my whole quest to understand the life and the universe wasn't biology it was astrophysics. In this chapter I will make smart people feel dumb and a bunch of people upset that I, with a library card, was able to understand and figure out their field that they portray as so complicated and near impossible to figure out. The problem, simple, they are religious. Antimatter and matter destroy themselves when in contact… really… do I have to be the one who points out it violates the first law of physics where matter can't be destroyed?!?! Are you "scientist" even thinking? You can't even figure out what makes up light or influences color but you know for a fact gravity is the weakest force, I don't see light turning solar systems or galaxies. You believe dark is the opposite of light and dark matter is your answer to this… holy shit guys, wow… you just found gravity. Morons, did you ever wonder why light is attracted to gravity… could it be their opposite polarities??

When I became an electrician I wanted to learn why we, in the meter, connected the neutrals to the grounding rods that went 6ft into the ground. I thought, "If energy is not destroyed, how are we running out and why can't it be recycled?" Physics books of today could not tell me really what exactly energy was besides electrons in a unified wave motion. That didn't make sense since light was viewed as energy without a polarity and thus had no opposite… so I looked to the sun for answers. First I needed to classify energy by certain properties tied to its polarity. Each moves or manipulates matter but two things I did find separated them into different polarities, their effects on matter and how they are emitted from their sources. Is it a coincidence a solar system and an atom or a hurricane and a galaxy look and act almost exactly alike… not in the slightest but what is that telling us? Well it tells us is how light is created, what happens to it when it hits matter and the ultimate result of its opposite… how? Physics books will explain how nuclear fusion occurs to hydrogen inside the sun… heat and pressure… that was easy… but it does not explain how fission happens to helium on its surface, why a star can form a red giant or how it can explode or how it's a self-sustaining energy source. My breakthrough came when I learned microwaving a helium balloon creates plasma. Microwaves work by energizing thin metal fins and attracting static electrons from the air to the point of creating a microwave by compressing them. In compressed gas, a microwave would cause friction from atoms vibrating against each other, thereby radiating electron and causing an ionic plasma state of matter which is what a star is made of.

In an atom there are two polarities; Positive – large, stationary, in the center and Negative – small, in motion and circle's around... applying this to a solar system is where I found lights opposite, gravity, I was amazed on what I found. A solar system has a large stationary object in the center with smaller objects rotating around it and each one had a force that could move or manipulate matter. The sun; its light emits away from its source and when it contacts matter it expands its electrons by attraction and causes an increase in radiant electron heat, expanding the atoms electron orbits, thereby changing the matters state from solid to liquid to gas to plasma. Now what happens to light as the planets absorb it for light contains mass and a planet never increases its size from it so where would light go? Converted... into gravity but to understand this I needed to know what light was made of and it wasn't photons or quarks, the key was color. Answering the reason blue traveled differently than red I eventually solved from a fission bomb.

Upon detonation, there are two primary events that occur and are the most devastating in a nuclear bomb... the neutron shock wave and the nanoseconds it takes to go from 0 - 10,000 degrees from light as bright as the sun, this was my first clues. Take hydrogen for example which has one of each subatomic particle, a Proton, Neutron and Electron. Much like a game of pool with a cue ball hitting another ball, shooting a neutron at the center of a nucleus will cause other neutrons to break orbit and hit other molecule's neutrons in a chain reaction. The neutron's inability to be effected from the subatomic polarities is what makes the neutron shockwave so destructive and powerful by plowing thru nucleus after nucleus with little resistance. After the neutrons are all gone, what is left of the original hydrogen atom is a single proton and electron... who would be attracted to each other. A neutron particle in the nucleus is needed to increase resistance from a negative amperage imbalance from the electrons motions to the stationary proton. By increasing the density without adding additional energy maintains stability however without a neutron the electron in motion would attract to the nucleus... until they touch. When an electron hits a proton, they lock and the electrons circular momentum it's transferred to a wobbled state from proton's added mass on one side. This causes a downward spiral trajectory and based on the amount of electrons bonded to the proton determines the wavelength of light. Light doesn't actually travel in a "wave" form, it's perceived that way, and it travels in a downward spiral motion that appears on its side as a wave.

Gravity, the thing Hawkins and Einstein could never get, I did in 2 years and created a fusion/fission reactor where compressed returned energy is used like microwaves to control and maintain the plasma sphere which also contains it from the microwaves EMF making it a self-sustaining energy source. It was designed after how the sun works and maintains. Science will tell you compress, hot, ionized hydrogen atoms will join together in fusion making helium... duh... so genius how did nuclear fission occur to helium on the stars surface again? They say fusion inside the suns core creates light which then travels through the entire sun only to escape out and reach earth... really... in the detonation of a nuclear bomb a neutron is used to split the middle of the atom that causes its destruction, what is the first reaction witnessed after its set off? A light so bright it vaporizes everything it touches real close. Still think light comes from fusion?? Light is the result of the breakdown of an atomic structure by removing the neutrons to where the electrons get too close to the protons and they eventually lock onto each other. The electrons momentum is diverted to a wobbled pattern from a circular one due to its increased mass on one side thereby causing a forward motion instead of a disk shaped orbit. Depending on the amount of electrons bonded to a proton determines its broad or narrow wave patterns. When you split an atoms nucleus down the center light is produced going in two primaries opposite directions... $E=MC^2$... should be Atomic Fission=MC^2. Did you know light was the opposite of gravity? Or that light isn't really a creator but a destroyer as it breaks down the bonds of elements and molecules. Gravity is the creator by compressing matter until the bonds of positive and negative are stripped and neutrons are able to be used again in an atomic structure.

Gravity... is a little more complex than light. Einstein wasn't even close, nor was Hawkins, honestly I believe our concept of a black hole came from Looney Tunes and their Acme "going through walls" black hole product. That's where we messed up right there and is why Relativity broke down as matter would approach the singularity point beyond the event horizon, because a black hole isn't one disk, its two disks rotating side by side. Think of two records about an inch away as gravity starts on the outside, rotates inward until it reaches the center and once there its trajectory changes from a X axis to a Y axis, rotates downward in a circle pattern making a cone shape and it reaches the outskirts and begins rotating inward again. At the center of a black hole, where did you think the matter went? Best example is a planet's gravity, let's take Earth. Did you know Earth isn't actually a complete sphere? That around the equator it actually sticks out further than the northern and southern hemispheres and interestingly enough you weigh less on the equator than anywhere else on the planet... why is this? Because as gravity emits from the poles and trickles downward in a circular motion and meets in the middle where, from have the same polarities, the two disk repel away bending outward and causing the bulge in earths middle section. It is also why at the poles a compass will spin like a clock because it's sensing gravity spinning around. Gravity pull is a misinterpretation; gravity pushes matter from the repulsion against its election shell to gravity and is why towards the core of a planet the gravity is "thicker".

Honestly guys, did you ever think "Well if gravity emits from the ground and pulls matter back down, #1 what is forcing it back down and #2 as it pulls down wouldn't it hit new emerging gravity coming up? A black hole is not really a black hole nor is it a doorway or wormhole to another anything. They are 2 rotating disk shaped collection of collapsed matter or atoms without neutrons where the proton to electron ratio is 1 to 12. As nebulas drift through space (a collection of atoms is a gas and solid states suspended in space) they will find a black hole and as it does the BH begins to slowly push the nebula along a spiraled track headed towards the middle, like a record playing music. The two disks compress the matter, flattening and decreasing its size, adding pressure as it approaches the center, thereby increasing its velocity and density. Once at the center, the nebula begins to spit out the "north" and "south" poles of the BH.

Now how it achieves nuclear fusion is the nebula inflow ratio has to be dramatically higher to its outflow and creating a pancake effect squeezing the core even tighter... until... the atoms get to close and fusion occurs first which releases the neutrons and makes them atomic wreaking balls where in just mere nanoseconds after fusion the neutrons cause fission but do not emit a shock wave for the BH contains it to the center and a star is born. Want to know what a BH looks like; look at the formation of a solar system. Galaxies are very similar only on a much larger scale. Advanced research into this I've done suggest mini BH within a BH based upon its size and density but is where a solar system gets its amount of planets and sets their tracks. Think of it like the cores of the planets are being pulled and not the outsides. Other planetary or solar gravitational effects can alter the trajectory of the planets but the tracks, planetary size and distance are predetermined from the density of the BH. How did I come up with this you may wonder, easy… our moon. As a planet size meteor sideswiped earth and knocking a chunk off creating our moon, earth should of broke orbit and sailed towards the sun… but it didn't, it stayed its course and sent it on a wobble suggesting that the core is what's moving earth around the sun and an outside force is unable to break its course.

# Omega

So there you go, I just explained how life began, its uses for sensory awareness for environmental interactions, how retaining those senses will construct a personality which determines their perceptions of the world from the intensity levels registered; leading to a rise of primates from a devastated planet rid of all its carnivores and allowing these tree dwellers to flourish. Then how a certain group was chased into a different environment, resulting in their assailants deaths from there evolution into the sapient super predators. Migrating across the world only to settle in a valley that was sitting in the middle of a gigantic fault line about to snap, which does and nearly wipes out an entire species in a few hours. Those to survive were a few groups separated completely from each other. Forced to reason magical beings caused their demise from Eden after seeking knowledge beyond their current comprehension and leading to a system designed to benefit a few at the expense of the rest. A war between religions led the world we know today and the vices we have which eventually will destroy us all. One possible way to avoid destruction and head towards prosperity but changing our thinking is absurd for life is far too magical to have any control over fate from the choices we choose to make.

Evolving the gene's from dioxide osmosis, was classic, you can't say I made that up but my goal here is not anger or spite I want so much more. Yes I want the destruction of religion but from the benefits enriching all humans as smart as the rest, no more separations. I want people to educate themselves, I see it in them they want to. I want us to start taking responsibility for our own actions to ourselves, others and this world. There is no fairy cloud guy waiting for us to come to him or if we wait long enough he'll end up killing us. There is no horned guy with a shovel in the middle of the desert putting bones in the ground hoping it will make you think the earth is older than 12,000 years. The problems we face today are from our own design. I can't leave this world unless I tried to help it first so mine and all of your children have a secure and prosperous future and not one where they are ripping themselves apart from money or religion. So we came from chimps, what does it matter? I can think of a lot worse things to be from, like worms or mud for example. Don't get me wrong, i love humanity and I see such greatness in this species. Just as carnivores are dominate, intelligent herbivores are rare and we must remember that. This was the only way I knew I could get through, fighting wasn't going to do it. It's time for our species to rise above what we are today and be HUMANS!! This is stupid, we are so much better than we know. I didn't want to be the one to tell everyone god is a lie, I just wanted a future for our species and my children's children. As we claim such higher intelligence, from my studies on life it appears we are not. The smallest of the insects is the only one I have found to work together as one single unit able to accomplish anything, the ants. I don't know what else to say except good luck to us all, I'm not sure how the world will take this book or my insane simple reasoning but I just might be right. All I know is what we have now is not reality, we need to wake up and face the fact we are alone and the short time we have in life is all we get.

One last thing, as an American to the rest of the world... I'm sorry. I am sorry for how my country has treated the world when we have issues of our own as well. We lost control of our country long ago and I don't believe we will regain that back. My point is simple; our country's actions towards the world are not of the peoples wishes anymore but of a monetary agenda of others is what motives America today. We pay taxes on tea in Boston, have no honor anymore and expect a system designed on commerce, which failed by corruption, to prosper and not repeat the same action. I leave with a quote from Woodrow Wilson in describing our country, thank you all for reading...

"We have come to be one of the worst ruled, one of the most completely controlled and dominated governments in the civilized world – no government by free opinion, no longer a government by conviction and the vote of the majority, but by the opinion and the duress of small groups of dominate men."

<u>The only fate we will have is from the choice we make for ourselves</u>

Mike Lanning

www.ingramcontent.com/pod-product-compliance
Lightning Source LLC
Chambersburg PA
CBHW051814170526
45167CB00005B/2008